The Way
of Generativity

Benjamin Smith
Nathan Senge
Chuck Peters

ISBN: 1548610518
ISBN-13: 978-1548610517

CONTENTS

INTRODUCTION

> Struggles of the new paradigm

People around the world are experimenting with how to enliven their communities, organizations, and institutions. With greater participation, with greater wisdom, with more fun, in tune with the living systems that make up our Earth.

Many feel deeply and personally called to take part in this experimentation in one way or another. We are exploring new forms of work and economy, just as we are trying to find new ways to live with our Earth and searching for more life-giving ways to educate our children.

Direct democracy, engaged citizenship, generative journalism, community building, conscious capitalism, solutions journalism, open government, new narrative arts, the sharing economy – over time it has become clear that together these practices outline the emergence of a new paradigm many sense and some are living into. This new paradigm has been given many names; philosopher Joanna Macy and economist David Korten call it the Great Turning, historian Thomas Berry and psychologist Bill Plotkin – the Great Work; others have called it the Great Transition.

In spite of the broad recognition that a global shift in culture, economics, education, and politics is underway, it has also become clear that the individual manifestations of this new paradigm are struggling to find fertile soil in which to grow and thrive. Over the past decades, we – the authors of this document and our fellow colleagues – have gathered extensive experience in organizational development, systems theory, community development, management theory and practice, literary arts and media, and academic discourse. And we have witnessed a sad pattern. We have seen far too many initiatives started with great enthusiasm only to peter out slowly over time. Great ideas and detailed plans are left unmanifested. In fact, one colleague of ours coined a new phrase: PESD - post-ecstatic stress disorder. The ecstasy comes from the feelings of connection and possibility so salient at community events. But this is an ecstasy that quickly dissipates, only to be followed by an equally deep disappointment at how little actually then happens.

Why is it that we are witnessing the spontaneous emergence of these communities and yet they often fail to thrive? Why does the energy of authentic community work so often germinate and sprout vigorously only to die before it can fruit?

Of course there must be many reasons why the emergence of this new paradigm is being hindered. The complexity and interconnection of what we call reality is far too deep to allow for simple answers. But our experience in this work over the past decades has revealed one important aspect we think has been overlooked: generative community building.

To continue with the garden analogy, these new ideas and initiatives are very much like young seeds germinating and sprouting in soil that is ill prepared. Although their impulse is sound, too many manifestations of the new paradigm lack the supportive conditions for their flourishing.

Generative community building is the work of nurturing those conditions so that communities can thrive.

Community, in our understanding, is defined much more broadly than is common. For us, a community is any group of people with a shared identity and purpose. Thus, for this work a community could include small task groups, individual companies, larger social systems such as school districts or regional healthcare providers, as well as non-profit organizations and their stakeholders.

Generative community is supported by five fundamental conditions:

> Connecting
> Grounding
> Informing
> Discussing
> Engaging

In connecting, community members build authentic and open relationships with one another, and form a community identity. In grounding, community members make their values and interests clear and explicit to one another. In informing, community members build a nuanced and cumulative understanding of where their community currently stands. Discussing is the process of collectively deciding what shared vision the community wants to manifest. Engaging, finally, is the practice of making that shared vision a reality today.

Nurturing generative communities means identifying which of the five conditions are already in place and which require attention. One core realization that we have made in learning from both successful and unsuccessful communities is the role played by the interaction of convening and narrating in the fulfillment of these conditions. Every generative community has in place practices of convening: gathering together in authentic communication, sharing values, and collectively deciding on next steps. And every generative community has practices of narrating: telling stories of success, recounting founding myths, and penning a vision of the future.

Communities are at their best when convening and narrating of this type mutually reinforce each other over time.

> What is a generative community?

The central question remains: what is a generative community?

Generative communities embody a way of being that nurtures individuals, groups, and their environment to grow into deep resonance with one another. Resonance occurs when the mind, heart, and will of every community member are accepted and speak to one another with their authentic voices. Resonance occurs when our thoughts, feelings, and desires are welcomed and invited into real conversation. We can speak to the world and the world speaks back.

If resonance is the essence of generativity, the difference between generative communities and non-generative ones is one of degree. Inspired in part by the architect and philosopher Christopher Alexander, we have found great utility in looking for patterns in communities that display and exude a sense of generativity. This search has led us to see several characteristics common to generative communities.

Connection

The members of generative communities feel a deep sense of belonging to their community. They feel genuine connection to those they work and live with. The relationships are built on the very same trust, openness, and acceptance that is normally found in healthy friendships. This does not mean that everyone is 'friends' or that the boundaries between professional and private lives necessarily disappear, but that community members meet each other as whole people, with life histories, values, wishes, and cares that fundamentally affect the work of every community they participate in. As a result, members of generative communities develop deep, authentic relationships that seem to occupy some middle ground between superficial professional relationships and private friendships. This difference creates a very distinct feel to generative communities that is easily palpable. As Chuck Peters has said many times, when you walk into a place like this, "you can just feel it."

Internal synergy

Individuals in generative communities work and interact with one another on the basis of collaboration and mutual support. The default assumption is that each individual has a wellspring of unique gifts and talents that they can develop to the benefit of their own growth and that of the larger community. Each person, each skill, each resource, each opportunity is openly accepted in the community, which actively works to put each 'piece' into a synergistic relation with all others. The synergy comes from the constructive conversations community members have with one another as they take on projects together that lend themselves to their unique skillsets, and unique fusions of those skillsets. This internal synergy within generative communities encourages creativity and innovation, quickly seizes on new opportunities, while allowing individuals to grow in their own way. As the activities of the community evolve, members naturally modulate their tasks so that they each remain best engaged. Because of this, they can continue to grow over time.

This fosters a sense of ongoing, communal honoring of individual potential in which community members can self-select what they want to take on next.

Systemic synergy

Generative communities create this dynamic synergy not only within themselves, but also with all other stakeholders that form their 'environment.' Instead of competing with other communities and external stakeholders – competing with other organizations, fighting other municipalities for tax revenue, pressuring suppliers to lower prices, and fighting to survive, generally – generative communities see their own health and vibrancy as fully interconnected with those communities and stakeholders that surround them. With this knowledge, they work to form mutually beneficial synergies as a larger system in just the way they seek these synergies internally. The communities themselves each have unique skillsets, just as their members do, and they forge constructive relationships with other communities around them. Generative communities are less attached to the ways they have historically done things and are instead focused on growing and strengthening the community amidst any and all changing environmental conditions. As the biologist Humberto Maturana said, "a healthy organism co-evolves with its niche." In this way, generative communities are particularly skilled at sensing new ways to interact with other communities and stakeholders in order to uncover mutual synergies.

Distributed power

The control of resources and ability to make decisions is widely distributed in generative communities, forming a major break from top-down hierarchical organizations. This distribution of power is in part related to the open and trusting relationships that make up such communities; there is simply no need to centralize control over resources and decisions in a few individuals. But it is also vital to their drive to remain nimble in responding to changing conditions whether large or small, thus avoiding the cost and time needed for lengthy approval processes. It avoids the rigidity of directives and instead functions by way of collective adaptation. And while the details of how power is distributed vary – pure self-management, the "advice process," Agile, etc. – generative communities support the agency and self-efficacy of all members.

Positive affective environment

Generative communities are not only different in how they are organized, but also in their affective environment: it just feels good to be there. At a more philosophical level, one could say that this difference is a result of each member being treated as an end and not a means. No person, no department, no group, no stakeholder is instrumentalized in the pursuit of the community's goals. Instead, each is given the same care and respect as every other. At a more immediate, emotional level, generative communities exude a feeling of mutual support, genuine care for others, respect and openness, humor, and, at times, even joy. People like being there, because the larger "purpose" of the community is an embodiment of all the individual drives of the members. There's a clear sense that the work of the community is deeply worthwhile, while simultaneously honoring the diversity of purpose within.

Whole people participate in whole communities in resonance with the whole of creation.

Generative vs. non-generative communities

Generative communities	Non-generative communities
Driven by belonging and opportunity	Driven by fear and protection
Dynamic roles within community, responsive to current projects and sense of potential	Static roles within the community, defined by hierarchy
Members feel strong personal connections; person-to-person relationships	Members feel little personal connection to one another; instrumentalized relationships
Explicit discussion of values and interests, defined by all members	Community relies on values and interests defined implicitly or by community hierarchy
Community values the information from all members, and works to build a cumulative knowledge base available to all	Information flows are limited and controlled; knowledge within the community is not widely valued and shared
Discussions include numerous community members and stakeholders, who share the decision-making power	Discussions center around convincing leadership, which carries the ultimate decision-making power
Next steps are elicited from the entire community; community members self-select how to get engaged	Next steps are determined by community hierarchy, and delegated to other members
Community works in synergy with its environment: competitors, external partners, and stakeholders	Community often in conflict with its environment
Dynamic: focused on continually developing the roles of the community and its members in concert with the state of the environment	Static: focused on sustaining past ways of achieving results regardless of long-term effects or shifting environment
Open and collaborative	Protective and competitive
Structural maximization of natural talent and interest	Structural underutilization of natural talent and interest
Friendly and fun	Scary and boring
Oriented to serve the welfare of the whole community, each individual member, as well as interacting communities	Oriented to serve the values defined by a control-seeking community hierarchy
Sense of possibility, empowerment, and upward advance	Sense of dread and fighting to stay alive

> Who's this work for?

Our work in generative community is intended for communities, organizations, and institutions which sense the need for change, but are frustrated with the models they have encountered to date. In our experience, this has included schools, media organizations, regional economic development groups, non-profits, universities, organizational development efforts, as well as small municipalities, church communities, and working groups. To us, all of these groups are communities. While there are meaningful distinctions between *geographic communities* such as a municipality and *communities of practice* such as a school or a newsroom, the conditions that support generative community are the same.

We continue to meet individuals within these groups who are convinced of the need to shift to a new paradigm and have been unsuccessful in bringing about lasting change. Often they have tried a variety of means to spur change, to shift their own mindset or that of their colleagues, or set off on their own to start something new. Often the enthusiasm and potential with which these projects began did not translate into real success.

> Three theories of change

Generative community assumes a unique theory of change.

Over the past half century it is possible to see three major theories of change used in organizations, communities, and institutions. One such theory, which we could call **the consulting model**, has long been the dominant model in business, education, therapy, and many other domains. The consulting model relies on experts coming in, assessing the community as one example of a wider phenomenon, and recommending best practices that are intended to create the desired change. In this model an outsider is called upon under the assumptions that external experts know best, that the community itself has demonstrated its inability to solve its own problems, and that fixed "best practices" can be distilled from other instances and applied elsewhere with equal success. This is the realm of external auditors, consultants, experts, SWOT analysis, best practices, and recommendations in which the problems in a community are treated as symptoms to be cured.

By the 1980s and '90s several weaknesses of the consulting model had become apparent. Consultants were very expensive. Communities rarely implemented the best practices "with fidelity". There were frequent issues of self-sabotage. Initial enthusiasm quickly faded. Pioneers of a new theory of change, which we could call the **emergent-design model**, include Harrison Owen's Open Space Technology, David Cooperrider's Appreciative Inquiry, Juanita Brown and David Isaacs' World Café, Peter Senge's incarnation of Bohm Dialogue, and, more recently, Otto Scharmer's Theory U. All of these radically shift the theory of change away from experts and consultants toward the community itself. The emergent-design model assumes that communities contain within themselves the expertise, knowledge, resources, care, and potential to solve their own problems and manifest a vision of a shared future. Most often these emergent design methods use set processes that lead a community through conversations, practices, and experiences designed to build authentic relationships that allow for the emergence of ideas and desires already present in the community itself. So while in the consulting model the prescriptions for health were given by an outside expert, in the emergent design model these prescriptions are generated from within.

In truth, we think that both of these theories of change have merit. If you have a steel bridge you don't want to rust, call in an expert on galvanization. Similarly, if you have a well-connected team that wants to design a new service, then emergent design processes can be ideal vehicles. But in both models what is sought for is a solution, an answer. In the consultant model, these solutions come from outside; in the emergent design model they come from within.

Why is it that neither model consistently leads to sustainable changes? Because the seeds that are planted fall on infertile ground. Because in both models too little attention is given to the foundational conditions required for any change to take root. Thus we are proposing a third theory of change, which we call the generative model.

A third theory of change, the **generative model**, shifts the focus from symptoms and solutions to the conditions of the system itself. While the emergent-design model took a step toward systems thinking by including all parts of the system in the design of something new, the generative model goes one step further and asks the question: what conditions must first be met within a community such that it is able to nurture the seeds that want to grow?

If we return to the garden metaphor, these three models can be very clearly seen. When someone calls for great tomatoes, the consulting model charges in with super, F1 hybrid seeds designed to produce flawless, everything-resistant supermarket tomatoes - no questions asked. The emergent design model suggests that local heirloom seeds that have developed over the centuries within a certain region will be far better suited to the particular conditions, culture, and soil of place, since that is their heritage. Finally, the generative model turns its attention squarely to the soil itself. It says that whatever seeds end up in the garden, they will require similar conditions to sprout, grow, and thrive. If we truly want all varieties to bear their best fruit, then we must first and foremost ensure that the soil – the conditions of thriving – are as healthy and supportive as they can be.

It's important to note, however, that the generative model is not necessarily a replacement for either model. Improving the soil conditions can function either as a sustaining mechanism to developments that have already been brought about through work with consultants or with emergent-design processes, or as simply preparing the soil for whatever is to come. Even if the soil is prepared well in our imaginary garden, we will still want some plants, whether of the super, F1 variety or the local heirloom kind. The work of generative community is about finding the dynamic balance between activity and receptivity, between planting the garden and letting the ecosystem develop naturally, between the direct intervention of the consultant model and the nurturing work of emergent design.

Thus, generative community focuses on these systemic conditions – above all, connection, grounding, informing, discussing, and engaging – as the most pragmatic and sustainable path to change. We can be but midwives to the paradigm that is emerging, but by ensuring the best possible conditions we can do a great deal to ease its birth and sustain its development.

The Five Conditions of Generativity

Connect Connecting is the process by which members of a community come to see and meet one another. In connecting the community is able to see itself, to see who else cares about a place or an issue or a practice. In the first instance, connecting involves the formation of communities and the founding of a shared identity.

Ground Grounding is the next key condition for nurturing community. In grounding, community members share and learn about what brings them to a community. Why do they care? Why are they willing to show up, virtually or in person? What are the values that ground their interest in this community?

Inform Informing is the process by which a community learns about its current situation in all its diversity and nuance. Informing is the activity of getting the best possible picture of a community from the macro to the micro. Only on the basis of a broad and detailed picture of the *now* can a community make wise decisions about how to make next steps.

Discuss Discussing is the collective practice of focusing the community on the precise paths it wants to take. Discussing involves inclusive and constructive practices that allow the community to share their visions of emergent understandings, whilst refining those views into concrete decisions about what to do next.

Engage Finally, engaging involves the concrete work of prototyping the vision arrived at in discussing. It means showing community members what they can do today, at a variety of engagement levels, in order to manifest their care about the community in real action.

> The how

How, then, can the conditions of generative community be nurtured?

A tomato plant can only bring forth its miraculous bounty if a sufficient number of complex and interrelating conditions are met over the course of a growing season. Plant the seeds in the cold of May and they will never germinate. Starve a transplant of needed water and nutrients, and it will wither and die. Withhold a full measure of sunlight and it will bear no fruit. It is only when all these conditions and many more are present to nurture the growth of the plant and its fruit that its full potential can be realized.

{
The key to consistently and reliably generative communities is an interplay of convening and narrating.
}

Generative community supports the emergence of the five key conditions necessary for the transformation of community potential into reality. To flourish, the tomato plant needs the support of an environment made up of many interrelated conditions. But the list of conditions is not endless. When certain key conditions are met, then it can bear forth across the globe from gardens in Iowa and balconies in Chicago to greenhouses in Spain and the wilds of the Galápagos Islands. Each unique, and yet each indisputably a tomato, dependent upon the same set of nurturing conditions.

Communities, as living systems, also depend on supportive conditions. Transformative ideas, strong relationships, skilled individuals, ample resources – none of these are sufficient *on their own* to bring forth potential within a community. Just like a garden, communities can only unlock their potential when a key set of five conditions are present and working in harmony to support each other. In addition, the conditions need not be built in order to nurture generativity; they are not sequential, nor are they ever finished.

> The interplay of convening and narrating

In the movement from connecting to engaging, we are moving down levels of abstraction toward concrete action. The generative theory describes how lasting change can manifest itself in a community by focusing on the five conditions. These conditions are those we have found present in all generative communities – where they are present we find communities able to bring about lasting change. But how do these conditions manifest in particular cases? How can individuals nurture these five conditions? Answer: through an interplay of convening and narrating – a central thesis of this work.

By convening, we mean those times when members of a community gather together – to get to know one another, to learn what they care about, to discuss what's going on. And by narrating we mean telling stories about what's working, about important events in our shared history, about valuable viewpoints from without.

For too long, the choice between convening and narrating has been an either/or. Community leaders, religious groups, non-profit discussions, town halls, facilitators, service organizations (Rotary, Masons, Scottish Rite, Kiwanis), as well as the conferences and meetings of the business world all focus on convening. As their main mode of action they choose to gather together, following set practices and rituals of convening. Religious groups use services with song, recitation, and prayer. Facilitators use practices like those found in the emergent-design model. Service organizations employ a cornucopia of collective meals, chanting, music, humor, and rituals. The business world, finally, tends to use conferences and meetings to discuss results, new findings, or plan next steps. What all these groups have in common is their focus on convening.

In contrast, newspapers, public-relations departments, government organizations, and academics have chosen narrative as their main mode of interacting with community. Media, of course, produces articles, stories, and broadcast pieces via print, video, and radio. Public-relations departments and government organizations rely on press releases and official statements: usually tightly crafted written narratives of their public positions. And academics focus their efforts on technical journal articles and books by which they interact with larger publics. Although very different types of communities, they all share a focus on narrative.

What we rarely find are communities that do both convening and narrating in conjunction with one another. This is to the great detriment of their potential generativity. The key to consistently and reliably generative communities is the ongoing interplay of convening and narrating. Either one alone – even if done exceptionally well – will not have the force of both done in combination. Therefore, the focus of a generative community involves bolstering connecting, grounding, informing, discussing, and engaging through a dynamic combination of convening and narrating. For each of the five conditions can be supported by both convening and narrating practices. For example, a community can deepen connection by gathering together and repeatedly answering well chosen questions such as "Who are you?" and "Why are you here?" At the same time, its degree of connectedness can be strengthened through the stories of individual members, which can yield a great insight into their unique lives and gifts. Informing can similarly be done by convening, such as when a generative-design process like Theory U draws on participants to map a stakeholder system. It can also be done through cumulative knowledge-building narratives like wikis. These are but a few of the many permutations by which convening and narrating can be used to nurture the five conditions essential to generative community.

Let us return one more time to the garden metaphor because, perhaps, it isn't a metaphor at all; it is simply a clear example of a living, generative community. Gardens are complex. There are numerous conditions that must be met for plants to thrive: water, light, soil nutrients, temperature, and so on. What's more, neglecting any one of them can damage the generativity of the whole garden. That's our read on generative communities as well. What we hope to add to the work of individuals and communities is an awareness of the fundamental conditions of generative community and an understanding of how various convening and narrating practices, working in tandem, can serve to nurture those conditions. The ultimate goal is to nurture communities in which these healthy conditions are strong, stable components of a soil capable of bearing whatever bounty is trying to emerge.

The ultimate goal is to nurture communities in which these healthy conditions are strong, stable components of a soil capable of bearing whatever bounty is trying to emerge.

The structure of this text

I   **The conditions of generative community**
The first chapter of the text goes into greater depth
describing the five conditions of generative community:
connecting, grounding, informing, discussing, and
engaging.

II   **The interplay of convening and narrating**
The second chapter describes both convening and
narrating as the twin dynamics of nurturing the
conditions of generative community. With ample
examples putting bones on the theory, the chapter also
sketches the essentials in using convening and narrating in
community.

III   **Individual skills of generative community**
While convening and narrating make up the core practices
in nurturing generative community, each of us as
individuals is also called upon to manifest our being in
community in ways that support generativity. While this is
a complex and unbounded field of exploration and
experimentation, a few core skills useful to all community
members are outlined in the chapter.

IV   **Measuring success**
The final chapter addresses the question of how to
measure success and progress in the work of building
generative community. Just because the time-scale is
often long and the conditions hard to measure
numerically doesn't mean that progress is a question for
the gods. Clear, qualitative questions for each of the
conditions of generative community can give us answers
about how we're doing.

V   **Appendix: Cosmology, and Why It Matters**
Generativity exists within a worldview, the basic premises
of which are not yet commonplace or common sense.
This chapter outlines the basic cosmology that undergirds
the rest of the work.

> The dance of heart and mind

Generative communities rest on two ways of knowing and being in the world: one of the heart and one of the mind. Care and understanding. Compassion and wisdom. Just like the interplay between convening and narrating, we believe this work requires both paired in an eternal dance.

The **work of the heart** involves authentic conversation, deep listening, good will, and inner calm that allow individuals and groups to "dig deep" into the core of their being, to speak about who they really are and what moves them at the most fundamental level. In other words, this is deeply personal work essential for community members doing their work and remaining honest about themselves. This is the micro level.

The **work of the mind** involves understanding the natural cycle communities go through as they live: connecting with one another, grounding themselves in their values, figuring out what issues are most pressing, discussing how they want to proceed as a community, and then actually manifesting those shared values and future in the world. Like carefully tending a garden over the seasons, this is analytical work requiring a systems view of the community in order to keep the whole on a healthy trajectory. This is the macro level.

Over the years, we've witnessed far too many efforts fail for a lack of interplay between the work of the heart and that of the mind. Too many community-building efforts, too many organizational change processes fall to one extreme or the other. Some are extremely genuine meetings of people passionate about an issue. Deep bonds are created and wisdom might even arise, but they tend to remain isolated incidents, unable to move their energy out into the wider community of which they are a part. The fruits of these connections fail to make it into larger circulation. This is the heart without the mind.

Others are wisely designed structures for getting the right people together, creating a systemic picture of the issue, and moving the whole group toward next steps, but they fail to connect with our core and thus lack the energy needed to push them toward full manifestation. This is the mind without heart.

In everything we do, we think that finding this interplay between the heart and mind, between compassion and wisdom, is essential. In fact, while this text focuses on developing a framework for understanding the conditions of generative community and providing a toolkit to nurture those conditions, we also believe that this work rests on a fundamentally different cosmology than the one that dominates our societies today.

Those readers who are interested in digging deeper into the cosmological underpinnings of this work are invited to look at the appendix we have written that provides those details: *Generative Cosmology, and Why it Matters.*

For now, we turn to the foundational framework of this work.

THE FIVE CONDITIONS OF GENERATIVITY

To date, communities, organizations, and institutions have addressed their problems much like a patient visiting a doctor; they identified a problem and sought a suitable solution. Within the mechanical cosmology that has dominated the West for centuries, this is common sense. A problem is like a faulty part of a machine. The dysfunction can be located and fixed, thus returning the machine to optimal functioning.

Have a rash? Here's a cream that will help you. Students have poor reading scores? There's a new research-based curriculum that will turn them right around. Downtown looking abandoned? These five amenities are proven to bring people back.

What these approaches in communities as diverse as medicine, schools, and municipalities share is their search for a symptomatic solution – one that focuses on eradicating precisely the undesired effect. Ironically, the symptomatic approach has its own problem. Addressing symptoms, especially in complex systems like organizations and communities, usually fails to address the underlying cause. Symptomatic fixes might reduce the severity of a problem, but they rarely change the dynamics of the system such that the problem goes away forever. In the worst-case scenario, the ameliorated symptom actually allows the cause to worsen unnoticed.

18

(The reasons for this can be seen more clearly with a basic understanding of systems theory, which the interested reader can find in the appendix – *Generative Cosmology, and Why it Matters.*)

Take the example of reading scores. Teachers, classes, schools, districts, even whole nations are graded on how well kids can read at particular ages. These scores are then used to make weighty decisions about funding, teacher training, and curriculum choices. So when reading scores are low, something needs to be done. But what?

The symptomatic approach operates within the existing system and seeks a solution that will "fix" the problem directly. The problem: poor reading scores. The solution: boost reading scores.

The work of generative community is distinct because it focuses squarely on getting the conditions right. In contrast to the symptomatic approach, a systemic approach considers the entirety of a system, such as a school. Systems thinking assumes that all aspects of a system are fundamentally interrelated; it therefore goes against common sense to address a single aspect in isolation.

Generative community also addresses communities as interrelated wholes in which certain conditions are key to healthy development. Instead of prescribing a particular fix or best practices, generative community works by focusing on a set of five conditions that allow communities to flourish. In this, it focuses on improving the systemic health and strength of a community.

I. Connecting

The first condition of generative community is connection. This means answering the basic question: who are we?

On a superficial level, connecting is the very simple, practical step of figuring out who is present in a room, in an organization, in a community. Who's there? Are there positions in an organization that have been overlooked? What does the network look like? Who are the actors?

This is essential because having a systemic view of a community means having a reasonable grasp of its entire scope. Many communities, from small teams and organizations to entire institutions, fail to realize their potential for the simple reason that they don't know whom else belongs to them and what they have to contribute. For instance, the person you have shaken hands with for years but never actually asked what they did in the organization. This first level of connecting is, thus, about seeing who's really there.

But connecting also has a deeper level. This deeper level occurs when we are able to be our whole selves as individuals and as community members. Most communities, and certainly organizations, are not places that welcome all aspects of our being. They ask us to play our defined roles and pretend we are rational actors. In truth we are so much more – complex beings of emotions, desires, life roles, and ambitions. So, your predilection for stand-up comedy is welcome. Your golf game? Sure. Worries about your kids? Those too.

In this deeper level of connecting we collectively create an atmosphere in which such wholeness of the self is encouraged. When we do this we lay the foundations for the relationships that are the very material of the shift toward the generative communities we are witnessing today. So much of our energy is spent seeking connection with others and yet so often we forget this basic step. We can't do anything until we have connected with one another.

Think of an effective check-in. In La Paz, Mexico, we witnessed a group of fishermen trying to recover from a fishery's sudden and devastating collapse. They worked together with a nonprofit geared towards promoting sustainable aqua-culture, coming together each morning to discuss how they were going to conduct their day in the harbor. The check-in addressed how they were feeling and what roles each fisherman would play through the course of the morning, where they would place their crates of scallop seeds on the shoreline to optimize potential growth. Yes, this meeting had an immediately practical role in planning the day's activity, but it also played an essential role in building the relationships between the fishermen.

For the fishermen, this time building personal connection had several uses. Practically, they could assign their respective workloads for the day. If one person had had a particularly rough night (the region is highly impoverished), that person would take on a lighter task for the day. But it also gave them time to get to know their personal strengths and weaknesses, and thus make better collective choices as to who would do what. It also provided an opportunity for the fishermen to build personal relationships with one another; something often overlooked in businesses, organizations, and larger communities.

This is a place of hugely wasted potential. Spending time, regularly, to grow connected to our community members, to build personal relationships – relationships that can be very different from friendships – is not something that can be pushed to the side, relegated to small talk, chats over lunch, or an annual picnic. Connection deserves our regular attention because it results in us caring about our community and each other. We make greater effort, we dare to be more honest, we pay more attention, and we invest ourselves more fully in the community. Connecting is essential because it is how we grow to care about those around us and our community.

II. Grounding

The second condition of generative community is grounding. This means answering the basic question: why are we here?

While connecting is about being present and building a basic human bond, grounding practices take us to the core of what we care about. Most immediately, our care is embodied in our identity and our values. In theory, we could care about almost anything. We could care about activities like helping others, building great products, sharing joy through art, crafting useful texts, or fixing motorcycles. We could care about anyone: ourselves, our family, our culture, our eco-systems. And we could embody those cares in the world in a variety of values. For example, if we care about helping others we might try to embody compassion, patience, and respect. If we care about building great products then we might try to embody convenience, wonder, and simplicity.

But we cannot possibly care about everything.

In practice, we can only care about certain things. Each of us lives our life based on what we as individuals truly care about and the values we strive to embody. The very foundation of who we are as individuals is largely defined by what we do care about. It should thus be no surprise that we carry this identity and these values into the communities we are part of – our families, our professional circles, and beyond.

As a condition of generative community, grounding takes place when community members make their interests and values explicit, and share these with one another. Just like connecting, this means *regularly* taking time to lay out on the table what it is we really care about, why we show up in the first place. This could be done explicitly in an interview-style conversation, or simply through the content of a developing conversation, or around a round-table. And it may so happen that connecting and grounding happen all at once. There is no processual order to these conditions.

While this process of grounding might sound like something that only happens in philosophy seminars or Bible circles, it actually happens in our private lives all the time. In private we often speak directly about what we want to do with our lives and why. We help our children discover their passion and role in this world. We take part in discussions with friends about issues we're having difficulty with. We share photographs, movies, and stories that embody who and what we care about. In these and many other ways we directly share what we care about with others, and try to embody those values in private life.

For a variety of reasons, this kind of explicit talk about grounding, about what we care about and why, is less common in the public sphere. The demands of ever-increasing productivity seemingly rob us of the time to reflect on such questions. Cultural norms around the distinction between public and private life make these sensitive matters. Certain laws make discussions of values risky in professional situations. And good common sense seems to tell us that groups avoid unnecessary strife when some questions are left unasked.

But explicit connecting and grounding practices can in fact be deftly woven into the daily routines of public community life.

We worked for two years with a company in Berlin, Germany that helped nurture more connected organizational cultures. With a wide range of companies, from a large soft drink producer and a national publisher to an IT firm and a beer startup, the primary practice that we used both with clients and amongst ourselves was gathering in small groups (2-4 people) and taking turns answering the questions "Who am I?" and "Why am I here?" Each speaker was given four minutes of uninterrupted attention from the other group members and then received a minute of appreciative feedback from each listener. Thus, each working day began with this thirty-minute practice of connecting and grounding woven together.

By devoting a brief part of the working day to connecting and grounding, we created a working culture, a community in which we developed deep trust, knowledge, and acceptance of our coworkers. And by exploring our identities and values, we were also able as a group to align our interests in ways that significantly boosted the drive of the team as a whole. All this with two simple questions and the freedom to answer them as one sees fit.

In truth, this is all that grounding requires. Grounding is the simple, but necessary practice of making our interests and values explicit to ourselves and one another. This is not just a conversational custom. Grounding is a set of operational tools that are instrumental in digging into how we uncover our shared interests and embody our values. Once we know who we are and what we care about, then we can begin the work of the day.

III. Informing

The third condition of generative community is informing. This means answering the basic question: what's going on right now?

Informing involves surveying as much of the available information as possible given one's value system.

Now that I am here, and know what I care about, what am I seeing?

All communities exist to get things done. They care about certain activities and use their resources, skills, and talents to pursue those interests. Connecting and grounding are necessary foundational practices for building a healthy community system. But on their own, nothing gets done. Informing follows upon connecting and grounding, bringing the community face-to-face with their current state of affairs. Who are the stakeholders of the community? What issues need to be addressed? What dynamics has the system showcased lately? What global trends is the community enmeshed in?

All these questions and many more make up the work of informing: creating a nuanced picture of the community right now.

Informing is well known and developed in communities today. Municipalities have extensive systems for providing detailed information about public finances, census data, and political processes. Organizations and institutions, similarly, have complex processes for gathering data about sales, targets, and human resources, for compiling quarterly and annual reports, and for reviewing individual, team, and company performance.

But this doesn't mean that our current practices of informing are perfect. In fact, we feel that three critical aspects of constructive informing – nuance, diversity of voices, and the cumulative building of knowledge – are too often sorely lacking.

Regarding nuance, consider the questionable state of contemporary science journalism. Too often complexity of a scientific issue is watered down to make an easy sell and "pull" a reader in. Instead of providing readers with a fuller, accurate description of gravitational waves, for example, we are plied with vague metaphorical language about bendy, rubber mats. The urge to make informing accessible is understandable, but not when the result is distorting or downright misleading. There is, therefore, a tightrope to be walked. True informing is about preserving the integrity of information so that community members can make informed choices about the actions they will eventually take. And this requires nuance.

Informing practices also tend to include very limited numbers of voices. An annual report might be written by just one person, an economics article reported by a single journalist, a community update drafted by one designated author. Regardless of how well such informing is crafted, it necessarily presents a limited view. In contrast, nuanced information is almost always created by a large number of stakeholders. Whether in academic disciplines, in complex diplomatic situations, or in community-innovation processes, getting a full picture of what's happening requires a wide range of voices.

Finally, very few informing practices today are cumulative. That is, they lack processes for creating knowledge that builds upon itself. Newspaper articles are published and then forgotten. Every four years, journalists have to redraft articles about the Iowa caucuses or how the Electoral College works. Important information is provided at meetings only to disappear into the ether. Insights are exchanged in community discussions that never make it to the page. In short, many informing practices lack a way to capture essential information and use it to build a cumulative picture of where a community stands.

Thankfully, addressing these shortcomings needn't be complicated.

Let's go back to the fishermen in Mexico. After the check-in is complete, the first thing the fishermen do is go out into the water together to monitor the progress of the scallop seeds' development. How many have grown? Which crates are having trouble? Together, they make assessments as to what they have been able to achieve on a daily basis. If needed, they re-position the crates to promote scallop growth. Usually this involves a lot of disagreement, but because the fishermen have already built a relational foundation with one another through connecting and grounding, those initial disagreements often flow into group decisions that harness everyone's individual strengths and not just those of whomever is most outspoken. This give the reports they produce both nuance and the perspectives of multiple authors. And because they have a well-working team with a deep interest in achieving results – their livelihood depends on it – they make sure to check these reports with prior ones to ensure progress is being made. This guarantees that their reports are cumulative in nature.

So why not simply export this iterated technique to other communities? Well, most community data gathering processes are considerably larger and more complicated than the case of the La Paz scallop fishermen. In such cases building a complete picture of the community's data through nuanced, inclusive, and cumulative informing will require more than a few questions answered at the beginning of each day. Systems maps can provide a dynamic picture of how all the parts of such a community interrelate. Community wikis can be created and used to build a deep understanding of specific topics of shared importance. And updates, such as newsletters and reports, allow community members to stay abreast of where the community currently stands. Each community must determine what set of informing practices best fits its goals.

Connecting and grounding build high quality relationships within a community. Through informing practices a community can know the current state of affairs in order to better chart its path forward. Wherever that path leads.

IV. Discussing

The fourth condition of generative community is discussing. This involves open dialogue to co-create an answer to the question: what future do we want to build together?

Discussing is the process of making decisions. All the previous conditions prepare a community for this practice. In connecting and grounding, we've gone beyond superficial relationships. We are able to shift into another's shoes for a while and see how their viewpoint actually makes sense, even if it may not have originally. And in informing we've worked to build a systemic picture of the community as it stands today. While we present the conditions here as numbered and discrete, none of them is ever practiced to completion. Discussing, like all the other conditions, is always an ongoing practice that can be embodied in numerous ways.

Still, there comes a point where conversation shifts and participants are ready to engage. What are the steps that can lead to the future we want? What goals do we want to pursue? What opportunities call us forward? What future do we want to build together?

As with the other conditions, this practice is familiar from our everyday. Meetings in businesses, organizations, and schools discuss 'the next best step.' Similarly, in our personal lives, we might get up on a Saturday morning and talk with our friends or family about the choices we have before us. Do we go canoeing, watch some football, help at church, or fix the porch? Questions of 'what next' also exist on a longer time scale than a day or a week. For instance, when kids are born, when they move out of their parents' house, when an organization is rocked by internal shifts, or when communities face a recession – all of these experiences also call for a questioning of what path to take, whether for the next year or the next twenty.

The questions posed in discussing are obvious. Getting to answers is the hard part.

Discussing is the condition of generative community where conflict most often enters the scene. Connecting, grounding, and informing all focus on content that's hard to argue with. You can't deny who someone is, what they care about, or the perspective they provide on the community. However, when it comes to putting ideas on the table about where a community might want to move together – then the real friction starts. It is for this very reason that communities almost always have set practices for decision making to guide the process along. Indeed, there are many systems currently in place in different settings for conducting the process of discussing.

For instance, in traditional hierarchies such as schools, militaries, and corporations, plans for future action are developed by small groups while the final decision is clearly delegated to one person (or a board). Some innovative organizations, such as Zappos, use a self-management model often called 'the advice process.' According to this process, each individual within the community or organization is empowered to make any decision – whether related to their role or not – as long as they first seek advice from all other organization members who will be affected by the decision. In the generative-design model, typified by World Café and Open Space processes, groups collectively surface their vision of a preferred future and then break off into separate tables organized by ideas to which interested participants then migrate. Voting is thus achieved without an explicit, balloted process. Whereas in a consensus model, like on communes or juries, after a similar round of collective visioning, an explicit vote is taken and a single path forward is elected.

In short, there are many ways for communities to arrive at decisions. Which method is employed depends on the community or issue in question. For instance, time-sensitive decisions are poorly suited to longer processes such as World Café. Because it so often involves unanimity, the consensus model can too often be a barrier to trying out new things, leading to gridlock. However, when communities face longer-term questions, questions about 'the big picture,' it is essential that the entire community system is involved in both ideation and final decision making.

One example can be found in the development of a new train station in the Austrian city of Bregenz, the capital of the westernmost state of Vorarlberg. Long in need of a new train station, local city officials decided to act. The initial situation was already tense as the two main political parties were at odds about the project. But they were also convinced that community participation was a valuable contemporary political process and so designed a community survey to gather input. Unfortunately, the survey was so poorly constructed that it only led to more polarization between the two camps. Throwing up their hands, the local government decided to do it the old way – they hired an architecture firm and other experts to develop a plan without the community's involvement.

It was at this juncture that the Büro für Zukunftsfragen (Office for Future-Related Issues) – an office of the state government – approached the city to offer any help that might be desired. To their great surprise, both the municipal officials and the investors were interested in the idea of convening citizens to gather their ideas for the train station. Although they didn't know that the architects had almost finalized a plan, a council of 25 people chosen at random from the city gathered in 2008 to assess the plans. While the "experts" worried about the possible criticisms of the lay citizens, in fact the citizens' council largely approved the plan. But they also added something essential.

Situated between a lake and a mountainside, the train station and train tracks had always been a barrier between the two geographies – something the residents of Bregenz has long lamented. Pressed between the two geographies, the citizens wanted the new train station to finally link the city to the lake. Within just thirty minutes the citizens' council had made a small, but significant change to the plan, proposing an attractive pedestrian bridge to function as that link. In this way a combination of two processes – the formal municipal process and the citizens' council – resulted in a more comprehensive discussion and train station better suited to the city as a whole.

Thus, discussing, as a condition of generative community, is the process of determining what possible futures lay before a community and then deciding which is worth prototyping right now. Although there are many methods for generating these ideas and making final decisions, we believe it is essential for generative communities to use visioning processes that suspend egocentric positions and seek a systemic approach to the future. Similarly, we believe that the greatest potential for discussing comes when all community members are invited to participate in decision making, giving them true ownership.

Finally, in the process of discussing, initial goals may be modified according to the needs of the group. In this way, goal setting becomes a dynamic element of the discussing process. Like all the other conditions, there is no definitive end, but once a prototype has been decided upon, it's time to get into gear.

V. Engaging

The fifth condition of generative community is engaging. This means answering the question: how can we translate this vision into action today?

Once a community is working on engaging, they have a sense of who they are, what they care about, and what future they want to pursue given the current situation. Attention then turns to action. How will that vision manifest itself in the community? What concrete steps can be taken? What practices represent the new orientation the community has taken? All this is engaging.

At one level most communities have already developed practices of engagement. In many communities, organizations, and institutions, "next steps" are the ultimate goal of every meeting. Even if the other conditions are forgotten or neglected, time is allotted to set out the steps of engagement. In the mindset of productivity and growth, action is the ultimate value. Everything else – connectedness, meaning, sustainability – is just icing on the cake.

Of course, this isn't true across the board. There are also communities that do a very poor job of engaging. Journalism's interaction with its consumers generally does little to encourage and support engagement. Articles that outline a serious problem and point toward potential paths forward rarely give the reader a clear way to get engaged. Comment streams, which seem to invite such engagement, are left unedited and uncurated, like a dog's breakfast of civic input. Similarly, government organizations rarely point to concrete ways we can achieve shared political goals. Instead, they tend to rely on the pre-determined processes of elected representatives and official boards, rather than encouraging citizens to become truly engaged.

Regardless of whether communities already have engagement practices or not, few communities have good mechanisms for maximizing engagement. While members all care about their communities and goals, their care and interest is rarely translated into engagement that leverages the full range of resources, skills, and ideas latent within the community. The main reason is a lack of ownership. When community members feel that decisions are not their own, then they are rarely as invested in prototyping. Furthermore, when community members *do* want to get involved, but are only given a prescribed set of avenues, then both interest and innovation are inhibited.

There are four matters that contribute to effective engaging. First, generative communities ensure that all community members are aware of a full range of methods by which to get engaged. Instead of creating a master plan and delegating tasks to individuals, generative communities present community members with a menu of engagement options, leaving the individual the freedom to choose and do their own part. In short, all the ways to translate the vision into action that have already been developed are known to all and are there for the choosing. Second, generative communities keep an open invitation for all community members to contribute novel paths for action. More than just choosing from the menu à la carte, community members are encouraged to use their unique combination of skills, resources, and perspective to embody the community's vision in ways not yet seen. Third, generative communities encourage ownership above obedience in the process of translating vision into action. In other words, such communities value individuals who make the vision their own and find their own way to act it out, regardless of the "official plan." Finally, figuring out how best to get engaged in a community also requires knowing what others are already involved in. In this way individual community members can avoid redundancy and make their own contribution to boost current efforts.

While it might be shocking to see and embarrassing to admit that our communities often do such a poor job of these aspects of engaging, the remedies are apparent. Even communities that forego connecting and grounding are usually good at sensing constructive next steps. One easy step of engaging is just making them visible to all. What takes more time and patience is learning to trust the innovative impulses of community members and nurture a culture of ownership within a community. This takes diligence and time.

For example, a common model of effective engaging can be found in many local recycling efforts. A local government might use online and print media to show residents all the different ways they and their families can contribute to boosting the total percentage of recycled waste. At the same time, they make available social media channels for residents to share additional recycling tips with each other, thus providing an avenue for novel forms of engagement. Finally, the community's sense of ownership of the recycling effort is supported by a combination of traditional media, social media, community journalism pieces, and local awareness.

Engaging, as the final condition of generative community, brings us full circle: from meeting as connecting individuals right up through the shared work of informing and discussing and all the way to action. And we use the word "circle" deliberately. The work does not stop with engaging. It's just another beginning.

> The virtuous cycle of the five conditions

We have presented connecting, grounding, informing, discussing and engaging as the conditions of generative community. As we have tried to emphasize throughout the text, these are not intended as sequential steps. Yes, they do often occur in the order presented, as in many meetings. We gather, exchange small talk, state the matter of the day, discuss, and determine next steps. But the conditions also support one another in important ways beyond the sequential pattern. In order to fully grasp how the conditions operate, we think it essential to look at how they interrelate beyond the normal sequence.

The simplest way, we think, to envision the causal relationships between the five conditions is as a reinforcing feedback loop. A reinforcing feedback loop describes a relationship in a system in which changes of one element in a system lead to the strengthening of a second and then cycle back to reinforce the first. A simple example is seen in patterns of population growth. More new births eventually increase the number of reproductive individuals, thus leading to more new births. Until checked by environmental factors such as a lack of food, the growth continues to escalate. While not exactly the same type of causality, the same dynamic can be easily seen in social groups as well. Say a team is tackling a tough project. A couple people openly expressing pessimism about the project can hurt overall motivation and drive, thus hurting the team's performance. That in turn leads to more pessimism as the reinforcing feedback loop continues.

But this type of dynamic can also create a virtuous cycle, as we see in generative communities. Sound connecting can pave the road for an effective sharing of values. Having this level of connection and grounding present in a community can make for a thoroughly comprehensive review of the present situation the group now faces, leading them to make the most informed decisions possible. The positive atmosphere of the community boosts the motivation of individual members, thus driving better engagement.

Or, maybe a discussion around a key community topic goes very well. A diverse range of viewpoints are heard and incorporated into a shared vision of the future and the community decides to take concrete next steps. The success of that one discussion could powerfully motivate new community members to take part in the next discussion, thus increasing the diversity of the views represented.

In a similar manner, it would be possible to map out all of the interrelated causal relationships between the five conditions to show how they form numerous virtuous cycles to nurture more generativity in a given community. Every condition is a goal unto itself because each supports a value of generative community. In connection we honor presence, the mystery of being itself. In grounding we honor the values that create our world and bring us together in community. In informing we honor the search for knowledge, our longing for truth. In discussing we honor our will, both individual and collective. And in engaging we honor our ability to act. Thus each condition is an end unto itself because generative communities honor each of those five values. But the five conditions also form many virtuous, non-linear cycles, which reveals that they influence one another in ways beyond the order we have presented here.

THE INTERPLAY OF CONVENING AND NARRATING

> Introduction

When we first approached this work we came across many communities knowingly lacking in generativity, innovation, and connection. We met local communities that felt a deep disconnect with their fellow citizens and knew that it was hampering their work. We met people in schools and companies who had known for years that they needed to innovate, but somehow couldn't figure out how to get things in gear. Across the board we met communities that had tried promising programs, invited experts and consultants, only to find themselves largely back where they began. In other words, these communities sensed a need to build sustainable change and they wanted to do something about it.

And yet within these movements toward generativity we have noticed a curious tendency to forge new paths in one of two ways: either through convening or narrating.

Common examples of convening are found in town halls or other public meetings. Conferences of all kinds are primarily valued for their convening aspects more than their content. In a more recent development, many communities today draw inspiration and hope from novel convening practices that have emerged over the last half-century. Open Space, World Café,

32

Bohmian Dialogue, Theory U, and many others have paved the way in introducing authentic, generative convening practices that create powerful experiences in the moment, and often show communities what potential lies in their midst. These convening practices tap into our human need to be together, to get to know one another at a simple, personal level, and to have frank conversations. More than that, they also go past the comfortable superficiality of our daily interactions, tapping the desire to have deeper interactions around our values and visions for the future.

For example, in 2015, we witnessed how two highly skilled mediators – Peggy Holman and Teresa Posakony – employed a combination of these practices to bring together a highly diverse group of teachers, academics, and private-sector individuals to tackle the issue of literacy in U.S. K-12 schools. Over the course of three days, the group built strong personal connections, mapped out a shared understanding of the issue, and began to sketch out next steps. This kind of practice has blossomed in recent years, with more and more communities and organizations discovering the generative power of convening. But this is just one half of the story.

In contrast, we have encountered many other communities that choose to focus not on convening, but on storytelling and narrative as the path to change. The civic role of journalism in the 20th century can be seen in this context, as one prominent example. As the Fourth Estate, journalism uses storytelling to check facts, present diverse viewpoints, provide a public record, and uncover misdoings all in the service of a democratic citizenry, with a deep understanding of the power stories carry. More focused news outlets, such as Mother Jones or Yes!, also use narrative to further their causes by highlighting both abuse and stories of success.

Another use of narrative for change is generative journalism as developed by Peter Pula and Axiom News, in Peterborough, Canada. It seeks grass-roots stories from within companies, organizations, and communities looking for what's working, what's alive, what wants to be told. In so doing, it makes a contribution to the groups it works with by bringing new possibilities to light, highlighting the gifts and agency of all community members, and encouraging others to get engaged and share their stories too. And, in a broader sense, companies use narrative in the form of public relations and "communications," just as governments and nonprofits use narrative in the form of public education campaigns. All of these communities share a focus on the power of narrative to change their direction and dynamics.

This choice between convening and narrating, at first, seemed to be an either/or. People from the convening sphere noted that the amazing energy generated at their events often led to little engagement and actual work getting done. A great sense of connection and innovative ideas sprang forth, but rarely did this activity result in sustainable change. Similarly, people in the narrative sphere valued the wealth of information built through their storytelling and the discussions that ensued, but they lamented the lack of connection and ultimate engagement with one another. In other words, convening or narrating practices alone only addressed *some* of these communities' desire to change.

Why? We believe it is because few communities are harnessing the synergy of convening and narrating done in concert.

Perhaps it shouldn't surprise us that convening and narrating reveal themselves as the two foundational practices of generative community. Of course, until very recently, community required physical presence. Without mail, telephone, and Internet, it was only possible to be with people who were physically present: in our families, towns, work, or religious communities. Thus, in its most basic form, convening as coming together physically, being present with one another, has always been the first prerequisite of community.

Narrating, in turn, brings a second foundational practice. Humans are narrative animals. The identities we maintain, the projects we undertake, the groups we belong to all exist fundamentally as narratives that provide the meaning and purpose that are hallmarks of human existence. Who we are as individuals and who we are as communities is something constructed, practiced, and negotiated through the stories we tell and live.

As simple as it may seem on the surface, one major contribution of our work is to see the power in an ongoing interplay between convening and narrative. Together, convening and narrating create a dynamic that can be harnessed in supporting the five conditions of generative community in a way neither can on their own. In addressing convening and narrating in turn, we hope to make it clear what these practices are and how they can work to nurture the five conditions of generative community.

Having moved slowly through this text from the more abstract concept of generative community and then on to the conditions that can allow such communities to flourish, we now turn to their manifestation in practice. Convening and narrating are *how* generative community is practiced. Through an intentional use of convening and narrative, communities have a powerful set of tools by which to achieve the generativity, innovation, and connection they seek.

CONVENING

Convening happens when community members come together. We can come together in a myriad of ways. We come together when we have a meeting, when we share lunch, or when we visit a conference. We come together when we celebrate success or mourn tragedy. We even come together when we talk on the telephone or via video conference.

No matter how long we meet, how many people are involved, and, today, whether it happens in person or virtually, convening is a fundamental practice of being in community. As interactive conferences, retreats, and hosting practices have become more popular in recent decades, some want to reserve the term convening for these one-off gatherings of small-to-moderate numbers of individuals who focus over a day or two on a single topic, community, or social system. Just like our use of the word 'community' to include everything from municipalities and small businesses to communities of practice and large institutions, we also believe it most useful to see convening in a much larger light.

Convening happens, in our sense, when:

1. We gather together,
2. with a shared understanding of belonging to a common community,
3. and some purpose in mind.

We think it's important to see convening in this broader sense because it allows us to see the commonalities in many of our community practices. Instead of seeing a business meeting and an Open Space event as two very different things, we can see what they share. They share a basic structure and they share the potential to further support a community's conditions of generativity. Moreover, when we see this deep similarity between various types, we can begin to see the great potential in more everyday kinds of convening.

For example, most people who experience an emergent, community event come away with a renewed belief in the ability for people of all kinds to engage in deep conversations, to build trusting and caring relationships, and to see a community in a new light. Rarely, in contrast, is that how we feel when we come out of a weekly meeting. But that's not because that potential is not there.

All forms of convening – meetings, shared meals, conferences, celebrations, retreats, conversations, and events – share the same potential to naturally support generative community. When we see how convening can work in service of a generative community, then it becomes much easier to feel the value of the considerable time and effort we make to come together in our communities. And, more than that, when we see how convening can support the five conditions, we are also able to convene with clear intention and purpose.

> Functions of convening

We want to make very clear how convening relates to the five conditions of generative community; how generativity is practiced through convening. The five core convening functions are to:

> Connect community members,
> Ground them in shared identity and values,
> Inform themselves about the state of their community and share learning,
> Discuss what shared future they want to co-create, and
> Engage in prototyping the new.

How the Five Conditions are Embodied in Convening and Narrating

	Convening	Narrating
Connect	• one-on-one conversations to build relationships • seeing the community gathered to feel a sense of belonging • sharing stories • shared experience and celebration	• personal stories – written or spoken – build a sense of connection to other community members • accounts of community activities allow those present & absent to feel a connection to the community at large
Ground	• sharing of values and what brings individuals to the community • explicit group tools to surface values and mental models	• stories that reveal personal identity and values related to community • founding stories • community vocabulary reflects values
Inform	• sharing diverse viewpoints around topic • check-in & update practices • cultural expectation of open, honest conversation	• build cumulative stores of community knowledge around topics • community wikis • stories/content that provides an overview of current knowledge
Discuss	• large-scale emergence practices reveal community wishes (Open Space, Future Search, etc.) • use of emergence practices in small group sessions	• presentation of various key positions for community to assess • facilitated online discussion forums, dialogue maps, conversation diagrams
Engage	• surfacing all current ways to act on community issues • culture of engagement, ownership • "advice process" technique	• public lists/boards on how to get involved • use of social media to share engagement opportunities • community journalism outlining paths for action

The five conditions give community members a framework through which to view the community's health. Our contention is that all five conditions must be present for truly generative communities to develop and maintain a constructive dynamic. Thus, the five conditions function as a checklist to which community members can refer to see what is going well and what requires greater attention. Convening, in turn, can be used to practice each of the five conditions. It is through convening – as well as narrating – that the conditions are lived in community. Let's look at each one in practice.

{ *Generative communities clearly understand the vital importance of spending time together building and maintaining connectedness.* }

> Convening as connecting

Convening is the primary practice through which connection is nurtured. Connecting means knowing the people who make up the community at everything from the level of names and faces to deep personal relationships. Generative communities are easy to spot because one can clearly sense the quality of the connectedness between members. They know each other, they respect and trust each other, and they care for each other. As humans, the main way in which we build these connections is through personal exchanges with others because all communities were once based on physical togetherness. Being a community meant being together and this convening is where connecting happens most naturally.

We connect through convening in many ways. We connect physically when we sit around a table or in a circle of chairs. We connect when we exchange smiles, shake hands, or give a hug. We connect physically when we share a meal, go for a walk together, play music, dance, or play a game. And we often connect in convening through our words and expressions. We connect in saying hello or exchanging small talk at the beginning of the day. We connect in sharing our dreams and our difficulties. And we connect deeply when we delve into questions around who we are.

In all of our work on generative community, there is perhaps no more powerfully transformative practice than regular connecting done through convening. Communities that have regular connecting practices automatically take care of the other four conditions of generativity. When they share deep personal connections, then they care about each other's values (grounding). Knowing each other's identity and values naturally leads to curiosity to learn more about their lives and share knowledge that could be of use (informing). All these together generate discussions about how to live according to those values and goals as well as augment the drive to put them into practice (discussing and engaging).

While connecting happens in all communities, its true potential is only tapped when communities explicitly value it as a core community practice and continually work to deepen the quality of their connection.

Unfortunately, this is far too rare. Few communities see connecting as important as time spent planning, working, or reviewing. In fact the majority of time spent connecting is "fit in" somewhere, such as small talk before a meeting, over lunch, or in the evening after a conference. The very fact that most communities push connecting into the margins shows how little importance the practice is given.

Generative communities, in contrast, clearly understand the vital importance of spending time together building and maintaining connectedness. They have a clear sense of how it feels to be in a connected community – treasuring and guarding it. And they have regular practices to ensure connecting doesn't fall through the cracks, that it doesn't fall victim to the drive to "get things done" that can so easily fill up every minute.

Regular practices of convening that support connection can take many forms. Some teams make time to share lunch together. Some groups block off half a day a week for reflection and connection. Some communities have shared activities worked into their regular routines that ensure connection can grow. And others are very explicit about their connecting practices, building time into every convening session to ensure that the basis of connection is present and strong.

Moreover, generative communities understand that the connectedness built in our time spent together can have various qualities. Not all connecting is the same. Much of our connecting – small talk, coffee, a chat – could seem rather superficial. Yes, in those moments we are connecting with one another, learning to see the other as a whole individual, learning about their lives, their cares, and their dreams. But it rarely goes deep. It rarely touches on those things that really move us, the worries that consume our thought, the ambiguities of life we feel but are ill-equipped to express.

Generative communities, in contrast, have the daring to venture into these deeper, more vulnerable waters when they connect. In check-in practices, in connecting exercises, and in the depth of their interactions with one another, the members of generative communities have learned to look past the normal guardedness of public relationships and find the value and generativity in deeper relationships.

Convening has a central role in building the condition of connecting in communities. Their full potential, however, is only realized when communities make regular time for them and dare to venture into the power of deeper relationships.

> Convening as grounding

Convening is also a very effective practice for grounding, often occurring together with connecting. In grounding, community members delve deeper into the question why are we here?

Our drives, our interests, and our cares are the primary energy sources that guide our decisions that push us forward in our every act. Homo economicus was just wishful thinking. Yet, rarely do we take time to reflect on what interests and values ground us in the stream of life. And it's even rarer that we share them with others.

A provocative way of getting at these values and interests is to ask the question, "What would you give your life for?" Some answer family, others their country, or perhaps God or their art. Many have difficulty answering the question at all, thinking that it means, "What would I be willing to die for?" But death is only ours to lose. It's our life that we can give. Thus, in truth, we answer this question every day, all day long in the ways we chose to live. Just spent eight hours at work? Apparently, you're willing to give your life for your career and salary. Look after the kids all weekend? You're willing to give your life for your family. Just finished binge-watching a whole season of Game of Thrones? You get the idea.

Unlike connecting, which does happen in myriad ways in all communities, grounding is often absent. Of the five conditions of generative community, grounding gets the shortest shrift. In most cases, our reasons for showing up are simply assumed, if they're given any thought at all. The result is that we operate our communities in the dark of our other members' motivations, weakening all the other conditions of generativity.

We can recall working with the management team of a for-profit company on issues around community building, work that was interesting and produced some learning, but ultimately didn't get very far. Why? Well, one main reason was that we avoided any explicit grounding conversations. We were motivated by the wellbeing of the community as well as by an abstract interest in the work itself. The management team was, we surmise, primarily interested in community building as a potential way to turn around a slowly failing business unit.

In other words, we were there for very different reasons. All of which might have been alright, if we'd ever spoken about it. But we kept quiet out of fear we might not keep the contract for very long, and we imagine the management team kept its mouth shut out of the fear that they explicitly identify profit as their primary motive.

This is business as usual in most communities for which convening can be a major tonic. Generative communities that have regular, honest connecting practices are able to develop relationships characterized by trust and openness. It is in this space that grounding questions – Why are you here? What's important to you? What do you care most deeply about? – can be used when we gather together in community. What might feel odd at first quickly becomes a powerful, direct way to surface our individual and collective values.

Grounding ourselves also requires repetition. The truth is that asking these questions is far easier than answering them. Some of our values are clear and easy to express. Others we know well, but are afraid to speak out. Yet more are not even clear to us, appearing only as vague intuitions and inchoate feelings. Thus when we gather together and practice grounding, we are not just communicating with one another about what we value. We are also naming the truth that our own values, cares, and interests are more complicated than we would like to admit. And we are joining hands to venture into that thicket of discovery.

> Convening as informing

Informing is a very natural practice when communities gather together. When we meet friends and acquaintances, some of the very first questions are "How are you?" and "What's going on?" These are some of the most basic connecting and informing questions. The answers, though similarly informal, provide an update on what's most pressing right now, what projects and difficulties we are currently faced with. In other words, they function to inform others about our immediate state of affairs.

The regularity of this practice becomes evident when we meet up with someone we haven't seen in a long time. We feel the pressure to give an update of all the important things that have happened and are underway right now, while realizing that it's just too much to fit into the time. But the point is simply that when we get together with others from our communities, we all know the basic need to keep everyone informed.

In many communities this kind of informing takes place in meetings. Whether it's a company, a non-profit, a church congregation, or a local government, meetings are an effective convening practice in which information about the community is shared with other members.

Emergent-design processes – Theory U, Open Space, Future Search – also regularly engage in informing during their convening sessions. In these community gatherings, informing is often focused on gaining a better systemic under-standing of the entire community. In contrast to most classical meetings, these emergent-design practices recognize two important factors that boost the effectiveness of informing.

First, the practitioners understand that it is almost always better to have more people in the room than fewer. Small meetings of people higher in a community hierarchy can never have the wealth of skills and knowledge that a larger, more representative group has. Including viewpoints from throughout the entire community system significantly boosts the chance that a more comprehensive understanding can be achieved. In other words, they draw knowledge from the whole community when they inform.

Second, they grasp that a detailed understanding of a community is not only useful for community leaders, but that it can empower all members to act in more generative ways. Thus, they ensure that everyone has equal access to the highest level of understanding available. In other words, they share that holistic knowledge with the entire community.

Informing is fundamentally about creating generative feedback loops. Physical and biological systems have these feedback loops baked into them. But human communities have far less perfect feedback loops. In a company, a product might not be serving the needs of its users, and yet that knowledge will get stuck, failing to make it back to the product development team. This is how departments get rutted, and inadequate designs take root and receive annual modifications where the whole design should have been scrapped and re-worked.

By contrast, consider the non-profit, Norestre Sustenable, or NOS, located in La Paz, Mexico, which is dedicated to rejuvenating a failing fishery in the Ensenada de La Paz. Each morning, a group of employees from NOS, proportionately representative of its various departments, convenes in a circle to do an elaborate check-in. The check-in begins with simple connecting questions, such as 'how are you feeling today' and 'is there anything special on your mind?' These questions, seemingly simple, are far from trivial. Many times, as the surrounding Manglito fishing community is faced with mounting poverty, these questions usher forth tough responses, which then segue into re-iterations of why the employees value making the Ensenada a sustainable fishery again and reviving the struggling community. These responses lead quickly into informing matters, such as which particular parts of the effort deserves focus for that day. Do the aquaculture crates need to be re-stocked? Re-located? Do they need to consider additional ways of earning income until the aquaculture succeeds in restoring the bay's scallop population, such as working for the government by cleaning the bay? The group goes around the circle one-by-one, making sure every person's viewpoint is heard. In this way, the most pressing daily efforts are reviewed.

This level of informing can only happen when a high quality of relationships is first present. The staff at NOS is able to do this as a whole because they trust one another as employees. They all know one another. They know most of each other's families, at least a little bit, and something a good deal of their life stories. All their viewpoints are honored. Otherwise, they would not be working together on this critical issue. In this way, proper informing transitions cleanly into discussing and engagement, and also gives community members a worthy working context in which to continually re-forge their connectedness and shared values.

44

Informing practices in generative communities are like highly efficient markets. Knowledge of supply and demand, of what capital is available, of what trends are developing, of what pressures are on the horizon – all of these contributing factors are transparent. Similarly, generative communities demonstrate informing practices that communicate what's working and what's not, what skills and resources are available, what trends are on the rise. These are all important metrics when electing which paths to then take.

> Convening as discussing

Once current issues have clearly been put on the table, it is time for community members to select their points of focus. Which, of all the pressing issues currently before the community, do they devote their attention to and begin to discuss in earnest? Are there major points of disagreement that need to be addressed? What does the community sense as the next best step?

Often discussing takes the form of smaller groups formed out of the community at large that discuss specific issues they want to tackle. In most communities this is for the purely practical reason that it would be impossible to include everyone in one giant discussion. Moreover, it's rare that all the members of a community want to participate in such discussions. They are confident in both fragmenting deliberately for pragmatic purposes and in coming back together to discuss what they have achieved.

The precise format of such discussions can vary widely. In smaller groups, these discussions can be quite informal, steered by the whole group or facilitated by an individual from within. At another extreme, discussions in generative communities can follow highly formal practices led by a skilled facilitator. What they all share, however, is a set of core characteristics. An openness to viewpoints from throughout the entire community system as well as an openness to the outcome of the discussions. A suspension of hierarchy and the weight given to various viewpoints. A deep trust that the community's ability to generate understanding is superior to that of any individual, no matter how expert. A belief in collective intelligence. And a patience for clear views to unfold.

Consider a group of engineers that gathered at MIT in 2007. They were charged with creating an online simulation to demonstrate the impact of global warming. The dilemma was how to reach a non-specialist audience while remaining true to the science. The group began its discussion with a wide range of possible factors that could have been incorporated into the model: the nutrient cycles of the Earth, the human population explosion, advances in carbon sequestration technology, and numerous others. But including everything would have made the online presentation unwieldy and therefore ineffective.

The group worked toward the final model through multiple convenings over many weeks, during which they went around the room making arguments for the representation of various key issues. In these conversations, no one person dominated the flow of ideas. Each member of the group pitched their case for why their chosen issue should be the focus of the model. Each case was voiced without interruption and respectfully considered. The meeting would then wrap up with a summary in which it was asked, "Are there any commonalities to these proposals?" It was only over a series of two weeks of convening in this fashion that finally more and more people began to see that one issue was common to all, and that in addressing it all others could be addressed as well. This issue was the degree to which the temperature rise of the Earth lags behind increases in the concentration of atmospheric CO_2.

And the discussions revealed even more than just this one key issue. Upon reviewing numerous statements made by politicians, skeptical corporate leaders, and even environmental activists, the discussions also showed the community that this relationship between CO_2 and temperature was a major blind spot.

This example from MIT is but one of hundreds. Constructive discussions are one of the primary functions filled by convening. Discussion is a fluid, living practice that engages more than just our minds and mouths, but our whole being. For this reason, convening is the natural space in which generative community practice discussing.

> Convening as engaging

There comes a time when discussion ends and prototyping begins. In the above example, ultimately this design for the CO_2-temperature model was elected, and the design phase took over. It took repeated convenings to get this right, as there were initially great disagreements as to how the model should be presented. With a graph? With graphics? With animations? With great or small amounts of numerical data? With possible levers for players of the simulation to pull in order to test various assumptions? Some wanted a great amount of complexity, appealing to a crowd already more initiated to the issues at hand, arguing that they were the key stakeholders, and some wanted a great deal less, so as to appeal to neophytes as well as allow for the possibility for new leaders with fresh, unclouded understandings to arise.

Even though only one member of the team actually had the technical skill set to design the online prototype, the group's convening and conversational dynamics remained in reviewing the iterations of the design. This member would offer a draft of the design, and then, either remotely or in person at MIT again, members of the group would, without hierarchy, go around the room and offer commentary on the draft.

Usually, there was a pretty even split between those thinking the draft to be too detailed, with too many degrees of freedom for the audience to manipulate by way of levers, and thus obscuring the lesson at hand, and others who thought it too threadbare. A middle road was arrived at by interpolation, and the designer would then go about creating a next draft to meet those specs. This went on, by way of iterated drafts, until those desiring complexity and those desiring simplicity finally met, and this draft became the model. All throughout this process, no one member's opinion was valued intrinsically as more valuable than any other's, and thus the model ultimately embodied the best of everyone's opinion.

Ultimately, a middle path was steered, and a simple graph mapping temperature and CO_2 concentrations over time dominated the screen, with a single lever allowing the audience to select the rate of CO_2 emissions the human world contributed to the climate. The punch line was well delivered: if CO_2 concentrations went up, so did temperature. But if they stayed the same, temperature still went up for quite a long time. It was only in decreasing CO_2 concentrations that temperature nevertheless still went briefly up, then leveled off, and finally began to fall. And many climate scientists argue that it indeed must fall to prevent the disastrous runaway effects of melting sea ice and rising sea levels.

Thankfully, instead of producing woeful paralysis, the model was found to motivate its audience. People felt empowered knowing how the system worked. Sure, the goal was very difficult, but at least they knew what the goal was, and they knew which solutions were inadequate right off the bat. The model has been successfully used in forums involving world political leaders, Fortune 500 companies, and countless schools and universities. And it was only because the group found a healthy frequency and style of convening endemic to their own goals that they were able to deliver such an elegant tool.

NARRATING

A community is the stories its members tell. To be generative, a community must honor the narratives exchanged amongst its members. For many of these narratives embody the particular strengths and weaknesses of those members while simultaneously performing a wide array of functions; in valuing them we augment the community's potential. We are narrative beings, and as we walk into the paradigm of the 21st century, nothing will aid us so much as the stories and narratives that support that change.

> *As we walk into the paradigm of the 21st century, nothing will aid us so much as the stories and narratives that support change.*

In order to see why narrative is such a powerful agent in communities, it is illuminating to see what it does. We have become increasingly familiar with the understanding that humans live in the streams of many narratives, but what work do they actually accomplish?

Consider the following example offered by Deborah Sole and Daniel Gray Wilson of Harvard's Learning Innovations Laboratory. They recount a story from Xerox in the 1980s in which an anthropologist was hired to study the field service staff to look for ways to boost productivity. In the fashion typical of the field, the anthropologist followed the workers not just as they worked, but also on their breaks. She discovered that "the [Xerox tech reps] gather in common areas, like the local parts warehouse, hang around the coffee pot, and swap stories from the field. Whereas a "reengineer" would see this behavior as unproductive and to be eliminated, the anthropologist saw the exact opposite. The tech reps weren't slacking off; they were doing some of their most valuable work [...]. The tech reps weren't just repairing machines; they were also co-producing insights about how to repair machines better."

In other words, the tech reps were using these stories to communicate knowledge relevant to the community's goals. The tech reps had previously been isolated as independent workers, without any formal community of practice in which they could learn from each other's experience. Using their breaks to tell these stories might have looked initially like "idle time," but in fact it was a highly effective way of spreading contextual knowledge within the community.

In narrating to one another, these tech reps effectively contemplated how to do their job better by sharing stories from their experiences in the field. This is something no manager trying to optimize worker productivity could have had direct access to without the power of narratives.

Narratives allow our experiences to be, at least partially, *transported* between one another. And their advantage over numerical data is that they can *grip* – they can pull us into one another's experience by way of invitation and evocation, and not directive. In this way, they can foster bonds between storyteller and audience, and lead to unforeseeable developments that transform the community at large.

This example from Xerox makes clear the kind of power narrative can have. But, this is only one example. When we look more closely at what narratives can do, we come to see a wide range of essential functions they fill and yet are often ignored by most communities. Beyond communicating knowledge, narrative can also embody community values through tales of great success or failure. They can be a way to build personal connection, letting community members learn about who a person is, their history, and what they stand for. They can help community members gain greater contextual understanding of a complex issue in order to sense a path forward. And they can be an effective call-to-action, rallying the collective will of the community.

Narrative is not simply entertainment. It is not a nice packaging of content that can be simply written in a list, summed up in a memo, or put into a set of value statements. Those practitioners steeped in the interplay of narrative and community – shamans, griots, bards, novelists, priests – understand that narrative may rouse our passions, may engage our emotions, may plant itself deep into our psyche, may bring us into intimate contact with people and places far away, and for these very reasons it is essential to community.

> Narrative types

Just as convening comes in a variety of forms, so too is there a wide palette of narratives. Narrative encompasses all the ways in which a community communicates with itself. Although this may initially seem like a strange description, it is less so when we view a community as self-reproducing system sustained by the constant performance of knowledge, values, language, and identity. Narrative is the life-blood flowing through a community.

Narratives range from the fully-fledged story, complete with character development and the rise and fall of a plot, to information pamphlets, and everything in-between. Narratives include stories told over lunch, gossip about other community members, presentations, blog posts, reports, and emails. More than just the stories themselves, narrative also includes the kinds of language a community uses, its dialect: the words and phrases and the preferred kinds of speech acts.

In grasping this broad diversity of narratives we have found it useful to place them along two axes. The first axis extends from *evocative narratives* that appeal above all to our senses and emotions to *informational narratives* that convey facts and appeal to our rational side. The power of evocative narratives is their ability to draw the audience into a world, allow them to feel that world through their own imagination, and then draw their own conclusions later from what they have experienced while residing there. The power of informational narratives, in contrast, is to convey explicit instruction to achieve a defined end. Between these two extremes lies the great mass of narratives, blending the draw of emotion with the clarity of facts. But this is just one axis.

The other axis extends from *formal narratives* to the *informal*. Formal narratives are easy to spot: speeches, written reports, and presentations. These narratives are usually prepared, scheduled, and presented to a large audience, whether in person or through some medium. They usually exhibit a rehearsed spontaneity and can become part of a community's canon. At the other extreme, informal narratives include small talk, gossip, text messages, and online chats and comments – primarily live, ephemeral communication conveyed by word-of-mouth to a small number of individuals. These are not practiced in advance, and they are plentiful, if one listens. Finally, in between is a range of narratives such as email, meeting conversations, and memos that follow some points of formality and are generally addressed to groups of a moderate size.

These two axes – evocative/informational and formal/informal – outline a broad field within which a highly diverse set of narratives can be located. All points on this field are necessary and all serve different purposes in different contexts. For narrative, as the life-blood coursing through a community, fulfills many functions. The following eight narrative types are not intended as a comprehensive taxonomy, but as a tool to see clearly how narratives work to nurture the five conditions in generative communities.

1/ Springboard stories

Some stories are designed explicitly to foster a certain kind of change. They are aimed at galvanizing their audiences by offering a tale set in an analogous situation with just enough detail provided to spur a like-minded action in the home situation. Stephen Denning, a former World Bank director, focused attention on the power of narrative and storytelling in organizations beginning in 2000, analyzing the roles such stories play. One of these types he calls 'springboard stories.'

"A springboard story [...] has an impact not so much through transferring large amounts of information, as through catalyzing understanding. It can enable listeners to visualize from a story in one context what is involved in a large-scale transformation in an analogous context. It can enable them to grasp the idea as a whole not only very simply and quickly, but also is a non-threatening way. In effect, it invites them to see analogies from their own backgrounds, their own contexts, their own fields of expertise."

Denning's archetypal springboard story concerns a health worker in Kamana, Zambia, who "in June 1995 logged on to the Center for Disease Control Web site and got the answer to a question on how to treat malaria [...]. The example shows that medical expertise existing on a Web site in Atlanta can lead to low-cost sharing of know-how with a health worker in a rural area on the other side of the globe [...] if it can work there, then why can't it work on a very large scale – not just in health, but in all fields of expertise, across Zambia, across Africa, across the entire planet?"

These stories are usually most effective when performed, often by a more senior-level member of the community who delivers the story to a gathered audience. Denning believes that the vigor and engagement with which these stories are performed before a set audience is at least as important, if not more important, than how well the story itself is constructed. "My experience was that *storytelling*, more than *stories per se*, was having the impact. The look of the eye, the intonation of the voice, the way the body was held, the impact of a subtle pause, and my own response to the audience responses – all these aspects seemed to make an immense contribution to the meaning of a story for my audiences."

What makes these performances a *story*, vis-à-vis simple knowledge sharing, is that no definitive results are envisioned. Only understanding is grown. The results occur later, and are not explicitly foretold. This is the power of evocation. For no one, unless the task is quite definitive and limited, wants to simply *do* what they are told. People want to construct that for themselves, and implement it in a way that harnesses their unique skill set and life experience. It is because of this that, for larger tasks such as these, that information sharing cannot compete with stories. By contrast, in a generative community, these stories are the main motivational tools for activating new and deeper levels of both discussion and engagement.

2/ Stories of identity

Some core stories reinforce a community's identity, such as tales of leadership, origin stories, and communal responses to crisis. All of these function to cement a community's identity. In these stories, aesthetics and emotion are central to forging a strong bond between events and cultivating a shared sense of belonging, and are often recounted at key community gatherings.

At the cultural scale, we find stories like Genesis, Hopi creation myths, or the tales of the Greek gods. At the national level we find stories such as the French Revolution, Washington crossing the Potomac, and the Pilgrims' first Thanksgiving. At the scale of individual companies, we have similar stories such as Henry Ford's creation of the assembly line, Thomas Edison's indefatigable efforts to invent the light bulb, and Steve Jobs' and Steve Wozniak's founding of Apple Computers in a suburban garage.

But stories of identity can be even more everyday. For instance, when record-level floods hit Boulder, Colorado in the fall of 2013, causing unprecedented devastation across Boulder County, the impressive FEMA response times gave rise to a story that still galvanizes Boulder residents to the present day. While many homes were destroyed, countless people were saved, and the tragedy was transformed into a story of communal pride that still serves to augment a sense of regional identity and motivate it towards unified action amidst the onslaught of other disasters such as wildfires.

These stories are often performed, either to a set audience or as a personal recounting among community members. Moreover, stories of identity get their power from regular retelling. Over time these stories reach what Denning refers to as a critical mass of iterated tellings among community members that collectively sustains a sense of identity throughout a community's history, "beginning with a story told by one member of the group. Ideally that first story sparks another, which sparks another. If the process continues, group members develop a shared perspective that enables a sense of community to emerge naturally. The first story must be emotionally moving enough to unleash the narrative impulse in others and create a readiness to hear more stories." Stories of identity are central to generative communities for it is through them, in large part, that identity is continually created, negotiated, and maintained. These stories are the spaces in which we connect with one another *as a community* and through which we ground our community values.

3/ Morality tales

Stories can also embody a community's system of values, its sense of right and wrong. These can serve to remind community members of those values, to rehearse them, and to publicly recognize acts of either great virtue or vice.

Morality tales can be found in narratives as diverse as European nursery rhymes, the tales of the Brothers Grimm, the parable of David and Goliath, plays from Macbeth to The Crucible, and all the way to contemporary TV series like *Mad Men* and journalism delivering moral criticism of politicians and celebrities. And in a less formal manner, gossip is an everyday practice of such morality tales. These narratives have the greatest impact when embedded in an evocative story, drawing the audience into a sensorial world instead of preaching thou shalt and thou shalt not.

Consider the use of theater in ancient Greece. Sophocles's *Oedipus Rex* was a dramatically sound play in and of itself, and thus drew an engaged audience, but it also provided an explicit moral message to the community delineating acceptable familial behavior. In effect, it depicted an extreme case that set a societal boundary.

Anthropologists have long known that communities define themselves at least partially by what is *not* behaviorally acceptable. They need to know and at times re-affirm what they are *not* and what they do not stand for, in order to confirm those behaviors they *do* uphold. These kinds of narratives help define both sides of this boundary.

In generative community, morality stories primarily work to ground the members in the values and identity they share. They also can serve to connect community members, as sharing values often opens up secondary tales of one's life experiences during which those values were forged. And these stories, especially journalistic work and gossip, can turn attention to current issues related to the content of the story, thus spurring informing work as well.

4/ Context pieces

From time to time, communities also need a larger context in which to make sense of the morass of everyday details that flood our lives. These pieces make visible the workings of the larger systems in which community members live, offering a highly zoomed out where-are-we-now kind of picture so community members do not feel lost and powerless. While these narratives are much less frequent, they often allow a community to adjust their way of being to a changing environment, and sometimes involve prototyping a desired future.

Context pieces are familiar from political speeches like the State of the Union in the U.S. or party manifestos, creating a larger story in which current events are placed. Sermons and other religious texts often do much the same. Documentary films, college commencement speeches, newspaper editorials, and board meetings frequently belong to this type of narrative, providing a reference point against which future decisions are made. Most business presentations are context pieces designed to trace a plausible narrative of events for a relevant community of actors. And consider the role of Foreign Affairs vis-à-vis mainstream news in providing essays that contextualize the events the latter merely reports on. At times, editorials in mainstream papers can play this role as well. These kinds of narratives thus contribute heavily to a community's informing and discussing, and secondarily to engaging.

In modern societies, where communities can become quite large and stratified, this type of narrative can also help community members remain clear of the community contexts in which they live and work. For they may be members of multiple communities that are each large, complicated, and stratified, which can at times threaten the ability of community members to identify with their communities on a personal level – the kind of level that likely attracted them to those communities in the first place.

As the sociologist Max Weber keenly noted, when communities reach a certain size, stratification and inefficiency often creep in due to micro-managing, the saturation of communication channels, arbitrage of position creation, and the like. Fine print spirals out of control and the individual actors within the community, sinking into the details and specialized knowledge of their roles, slowly lose their grasp of the whole. This is where context pieces step in, pulling the individuals out of their limited perspectives, showing them the proverbial forest.

Consider the perennial pieces that arise in newspapers outlining how the Electoral College actually works during election time. Yes, we're all familiar with how we register and vote – the details closest to our position in the political system – but these pieces give us the larger con-text within which we operate.

Likewise, in recent times, *The Big Short* was a film that interpreted the real-estate market collapse of 2008. Moving beyond the daily deluge of details about credit-default swaps, LIBOR rates, and mortgage tranches, the film showed that, when viewed from a larger context, the mechanism of collapse was comprehensible by anyone who took the time to decode the deliberately obfuscatory verbiage of financial instruments.

While context pieces are less common than other narratives and usually require the expertise of someone with a sufficiently broad understanding to pen them, their role in supporting the generative conditions of informing and discussing cannot be overemphasized. Fostering generativity within and between communities requires members to avail themselves of the holistic understanding created by such narratives.

5/ Reminding us of what's important and why

In large communities, it's easy to get lost in the details, in the small contribution one individual makes to the community as a whole. Narratives about what's important and why can remind community members, when our roles might seem drudgerous or void of meaning, what that work may ultimately be contributing to. They suggest possible in-roads into the next round of vigorously engaging work, and justify the small tasks as necessary components of a community's continual growth while moving along that road.

These kinds of narratives might be more needed today than ever. We are often the members of many more communities these days; our memberships can be more provisional than in times past. These pieces remind us why we wanted to be engaged in those particular communities in the first place. They realign us with their meaning. They are direct counter-measures to the feeling of being on "autopilot," of simply going to work or to a particular community gathering merely because it's "what we do."

Part of the work done by these narratives involves returning community members to the ultimately personal nature of a certain community to which they belong. They remind us that a community is made up first and foremost of people, for large communities run the risk of dissolving into abstraction: "the company", "the city", "the movement." This can make us care less about them. Personal stories of some sort counter-balance this tendency. Oftentimes, a company's founding story will serve this kind of role – they can provide a refreshing look into the core need that drove the company's founder to create the company.

A company executive might write an impassioned blog post about how and why she founded the company. A politician might rally his electorate around a shared piece of ideology. Or a teacher might recount a personal story about the deep meaning of his work.

All of these narratives can remind us of what's important and why. These narratives offer specific and perhaps not-so-distant tales of success, of a specific goal the community recently set and met, to drive their next task. As narratives that reconnect us to one another and reground us in our shared values and identity, they are a direct counterweight to feelings of anonymity that might otherwise arise among community members.

6/ Address misconceptions

Complexity inherent in larger communities also often leads to misconceptions and destructive generalizations. These often become the basis for entrenched ways of thinking about community issues, thus leading to faulty importations of past solutions into a realm of genuinely new events. Past solutions are simply ushered into the present because "it's always how we've done things before."

This smacks of bureaucratic inertia and an undue faith on precedents. It also often results in the ossifications of specific departments and offices and how "they do things." Identifying these kinds of stagnant ways of doing and thinking becomes an empowering tool for community members, and unleashes their ability to see things anew and address the unique specifics of a novel situation. This kind of empowerment significantly bolsters the energy of a community and re-positions it in a state of perpetual growth. Failing to address these kinds of misconceptions, which when unaddressed often continue to re-emerge again and again and drive a community into a static loop of repetitive problem-solving and thus derail it from its movement through the five conditions. Indeed, these narratives thus primarily address informing and discussing.

7/ Reports

Sometimes the need for precise information, especially when confronted with a more specific, immediate task, trumps the urge for a knockout story. Enter the world of report narratives, which are closer to the 'information-sharing' end of the narrative spectrum, though some presence of evocative story may still remain. Reports are used to keep community members up-to-speed on important events from the recent past. In oral cultures, this can be done on a one-to-one basis; you simply identify who needs to know what and you tell them. In larger literate cultures, however, this is often done in the form of hard news, updates, and reports. In these narratives, concision and accuracy play a big role, and they hew closer to fact.

Governments widely use this form of narrative in departmental reports, censuses, and press conferences. A company's internal narrative work also focuses on reports outlining recent developments and data, especially those that pertain to where they stand on meeting their goals. Weather reports, business journalism, sports scores, and election results are all like-minded examples found in the media.

These kinds of reports can lead directly to communal discussion and action, to informing, discussing, and engaging. For instance, consider the small rural lake community of Lake Wauschacum in central Massachusetts, whose members noticed over time that algae growth in the lake was reaching unprecedented levels. The water had become murky and fish species were declining. Community members elected to consult town records on algae levels per annum and compare them with what they were seeing. In other words, they began with the facts.

Acquainting themselves with these facts, community members realized that the number of boats that could put in at the lake per day had to be limited. This resulted in a town meeting, a convening session, in which this was debated, and eventually an actual town ordinance, limiting lake usage to only those members of the town.

Note here that the subject of this report was deemed to be of critical importance to the community – *that* was the subjective lens through which that report was filtered and selected for community discussion amidst many other possibilities. In this sense, it is more common for 'community journalism' of this type to couple informing with discussing than in mainstream media, due to the closeness of the content to community members. They *care* about what the outcome of the story is – they are hardly content merely to give a story. The content of that story can be pivotal to the community's longevity.

8/ Archives, data & libraries

Finally, we move to the storehouses of pure data, which in and of themselves are purely information-based narratives bereft of story, though the information found therein may assist community members in constructing future stories. For communities often maintain archives of whatever data they find significant: names, dates, maps, stores, historical records, texts, and, well, almost everything they deem important. At one level these are stores of knowledge, while at another they also reveal what truly matters to a community.

Whereas reports often detail events of recent occurrence, archives tabulate a community's history, often so that precedents can be observed and alarming present-day deviations from those precedents can be noted. Consider the lake community again. How would community members aware of a serious systemic problem be able to *prove* their contentions to the rest of the community (say, those who do not live on the lake) without data from years past? Perhaps they would be able to appeal to the visual senses alone with comparative photographs, but the presence of data archives certainly makes the case much more quantifiable – which is nearly always preferred by any kind of governing board – and in that sense easier to make.

In the spirit of preserving a community's historical sense of tastes and values, archives also exist simply to store the great narratives of the past, or those works communities deem of sufficient value to save in order to be viewed again and again for either their intrinsic narrative strength or moralistic import. Indeed, it has been said that one could know the ancient Egyptians by noting what they stored in the libraries of Alexandria. What they had written down there was what they intended to endure, both as a source of pride, enjoyment, and possible moralistic guidance to succeeding generations and whomever was to discover them should their civilization one day fall. They serve to remind community members, and outsiders, of the core values for which a certain community stands.

A provisional typology

This typology of narratives is only provisional. It is meant to be provocative and not delimiting. Still, we are convinced that we can be much more effective in nurturing generative communities and learn much more about their process of development if we clarify the many ways different types of narratives can support community growth. It is also meant to highlight which types of narratives may help different types of communities in different realms of problems that they themselves will likely face, so as to not be overwhelmed with possible narrative options.

Narratives are not a panacea. They need to be woven in with convening in a constructive fashion in order to foster generativity over time. Especially when dealing with interpersonal issues, narratives can pave a road of connection that can lead to a later convening in which the resultant work is reflected upon and evaluated and woven into a narrative again. It can lead to what Denning calls "an understanding of the potential of the change idea [that] can erupt into the collective consciousness, producing a sudden coalescence of vision in the minds of the listeners."

These kinds of story-based narratives are essential in communities because overly directly explicating instructions to community members in an information-sharing-based way often makes recipients bored or, worse, offended. Stories offer *invitation*-based ways to proceed, engagingly activating recipients in co-constructing meaning thus making solutions their own. This may sacrifice a bit of planning outcomes in advance for emotional rallying power, but, when compared with effecting little change at all, this is often a satisfactory choice.

For some reason, this understanding has become clouded in many communities. As has the understanding that narrative stands not alone, but in a generative interplay with convening. The two work hand in hand, convening bringing us together in body and narrating bringing us together in spirit. When these two enter into a supporting dynamic, then communities are secure in the foundation of who they are and can allow for the characteristics of generativity to emerge. This is what has been forgotten: generative community is built on the continual interplay of convening and narrating.

THE 'HOW': ELEMENTS OF SUCCESS

The key to nurturing generative community lies in the interplay of convening and narrating, but that alone is not a recipe for success. Through numerous experiences, a number of elements of success have become clear, elements that must be paid sufficient attention if we as communities are not to fall back into our old patterns. Generative communities, when they are humming along, are strong, resilient systems. They have achieved a level of self-correcting behavior that can absorb dissonance and stay on course. But when they are growing, they are fragile - very fragile. And in almost every case we are dealing with new communities that sense a desire and need to grow into generativity. Like sensitive new seedlings, it's not just the basics of water and sunlight that we need to pay attention to. These elements of success require our attention just as much.

> Generative power dynamics

Even within an ongoing series of conversations and narrative activities, it's very easy for power dynamics to ruin everything. At the core of generative community is the freedom of each individual – person, dyad, team, group, department – to follow the energy and opportunities that draw them out. If this condition is not met, if it is *for any reason* not possible to provide this freedom to each individual, then the generative power of the community is seriously threatened, if not killed. The problem is that it is all too easy for power dynamics to hamper this condition. Great caution is needed.

The most common way in which power dynamics are skewed against generativity is by having a single, powerful institution host and fund the convening-narrating process. Whether it is a local city government or an individual company or a well-meaning non-profit organization, the outcome is the same. By having a single institution host and fund such a process, the implicit focus of the participants becomes oriented toward that same institution, and not the energy and potential of the participants, nor the wellbeing of the community at large. At every step of the way – who's invited, what values are trumpeted, the kind of information that is sought, the direction of the discussion, and how the participants move toward engagement – the free flow is inhibited through an often unconscious deference to what is perceived as the preferences of the hosting institution. Like visiting someone else's home, the tendency is always to defer to the house rules.

There's a glaring blind spot in common views about what constitutes productive power dynamics. We can clearly see the inefficiencies of Soviet-style central planning at the government level, such as incomplete information about the details of the system, inability to react quickly to changing conditions, system dynamics that sap motivation and personal engagement, unuseful benchmarks of success, and on, and on. And yet we're unable to see these same deleterious dynamics of centralized power in our communities and organizations.

Generative power dynamics does not imply the absence of power. There is always power distributed in the skills, resources, and knowledge wielded by community members. Generative power dynamics arise when the community moves away from central-planning-style practices towards those in which diverse members of a community meet on common ground (shared space), co-fund the convening-narrating process (shared practice), and collaborate on how to engage in the community (shared action). Often this is done through a third-party hosting organization, which can provide a point of reference from outside the system. It is done through convening practices that give all voices equal weight, and gives real ownership to all participants. It is essential for power dynamics to be truly distributed and collaborative if generativity is to emerge.

> Openness to outcome

Generativity requires a stubborn openness to outcomes. There can be no specific direction stated or implied at the outset. The space the community creates when it convenes must be open to all perspectives and directions. This is because the very nature of generativity is the openness to potential.

The problem is that potential is shy and delicate. In any community the dominant elements and dynamics are, by very definition, those with the greatest power. They take up the greatest resources, occupy the most space, dominate flows and practices. Even when a community agrees that some dynamic has become pathological, creating outcomes contrary to the values

{ *Generativity requires a stubborn openness to outcomes. This is because the very nature of generativity is the openness to potential.* }

and goals of the community, it often still continues to prevail, like weeds choking a garden bed.

Openness to outcome is like clearing the bed, turning the soil over so that new seedlings can sprout. In community this can be fostered in various ways. Generative power dynamics ensure that no single institution or community element "sets the agenda," implicitly or explicitly, for the work of the community. A diverse presence from community members ensures that the whole community system is present, not dominated by just one or two perspectives.

Connecting and grounding practices are a strong engine of openness as well. Individuals, groups, and communities can be hampered in their openness by the constricting definitions of their roles and the expectations those roles entail. When we see the CEO as a leader with access to resources, when we see "outsiders" as the source of criticism and discontent, when we see students as the ones who have nothing to teach, then we restrict the openness of the community for the individual and the whole. Connecting and grounding practices help us move beyond these roles and expectations into vulnerability. In becoming vulnerable, we lower our defenses. And when we do that, we are open to whatever arises in the community.

Finally, openness to outcome must also include the very real possibility that, for the moment at least, deeper connection and greater under-standing remain the only tangible results. When communities start down the road to generativity, there is often a stark deficit in the quality of these relationships and the level of community awareness. While the goal of generativity is ultimately to nurture a community capable to unleashing hidden potential in its everyday activities and practices, this is rarely the first step on that journey. Often simply fostering these relationships comes first, and sometimes this takes time.

> Genuine ownership

Getting the power dynamics within a community right for generativity essentially comes down to making sure that no one person or institution has too much power. The flip side of that same coin is that generativity also requires each individual and institution to step up the plate and live into the shared ownership of the community. Ownership isn't about property or possessions. It's not a legal designation. Ownership in generative community is both a mindset and a practice.

Unfortunately, the mindset of ownership has too often been systematically drummed out of us. Representative government takes away citizens' ownership of the political process and puts the responsibility in the hands of elected officials. The legal system takes away the mindset of shared ownership in businesses and organizations through its demand that someone be held legally accountable for misdeeds. In fact, hierarchies of all kinds deprive communities of their shared ownership by delineating the responsibilities of individual actors, thereby stripping all other community members of their felt responsibility. In other words, if it's the manager's job, then it ain't mine.

By contrast, in the mindset of ownership, every member of the community shares the responsibility for the outcomes it creates. There is no assumption that one person's position in the community thereby relinquishes all others from their responsibility. In a company, it's not a manager's fault if targets are not met; it's that of the CEO and the IT department and the board and so on. In a school, it's not the teachers' responsibility if the children fail to learn; it's the responsibility of every member of the school community.

For instance, St. George's Primary School, in Battersea, London, underwent just this kind of mindset shift when they began trying to turn around the once failing school. No longer were the teachers alone considered responsible for the kids' academic outcomes. Instead the school community made it explicit that the success of the children was the shared responsibility of everyone from the administration to the cleaning staff. And now the school ranks as one of the top schools in England.

The practice of ownership means more than just having a sense of shared responsibility, but acting on it as well. In real terms, this means that the members of generative communities draw on all their skills and resources when committing to community engagement. That is why it is essential to have practices of commitment as a core element of the convening-narrating process. By repeatedly asking community members what gifts they have to contribute, what steps they can commit to right now, and what they are willing to sacrifice for the community, members slowly grow into the mindset and practice of ownership. Commitment takes many forms: donating skills and time, joining project groups, creating narratives and art, taking care of the group, pooling funds. At the very least, participants commit to when they should meet again.

> Critical frequency

One convening is not enough. Nor is two. Nor even three. It's hard to overstate this point: generativity is not a product, it's an ongoing practice.

For several decades now most efforts to nurture generativity in communities have focused on single events that intended to provide a shot in the arm. The "difference that would make a difference." The silver bullet. Whether for a single day or more, once these events were over, they were *over*.

In other communities a pattern has developed of gathering once a year. And more recently some communities have begun experimenting with longer series of convening-narrating processes such as the Peterborough Dialogues (Canada, 2015-6) led by Axiom News, or the discussions around asylum seekers in the Austrian state of Vorarlberg (2015-2016) led by the Office for Future-Related Issues, a government agency.

These variations in how often communities convene reveal a clear conclusion: there is a 'critical frequency' of convening-narrating that must be reached and sustained for generativity to arise. Again, the five conditions of generative community are not products that can be carefully planned and executed. The conditions of generative community are dynamic processes that are practiced and maintained. They are verbs, not nouns.

In the garden metaphor, the acts of weeding, watering, and feeding convey a clear sense of this critical frequency. They needn't be done constantly. Too much is also detrimental. In excess they can "drown" the plant attempting to grow. But nor can they be done too infrequently, lest the soil dry out and the beds become choked with weeds.

Communities must convene together again and again to sustain their sense of connection and groundedness, to remain abreast of new information, to work through the issues that are pressing today, and make the next steps given current conditions. Narration, similarly, must be ongoing and repeated in its support of these community dynamics.

There can be no hard-and-fast rules about how frequently a community must convene or how much narration is enough. Each community is unique in far too many regards. But the basic fact remains that if convening and narrating are to nurture generativity in any sustainable way, these activities must be repeated at close to that community's critical frequency.

> Moderator

Having a moderator or a "host" is often crucial in these communal convenings for a number of reasons.

First, in overseeing recurrent convenings, moderators ensure that they do not run aground or become stale. There is an ongoing need for some slight variation in convening and narrating practices in order to sustain a feeling of freshness. Communities truly benefit from having someone outside their immediate circle, outside their system boundaries, to provide this fresh perspective and keep them moving along and deter a state of collective somnambulance. This often results in what Peter Pula calls "semi-unique" convenings. There is enough commonality between sessions to provide continuity, but enough difference to spur innovation.

Another purpose of the moderator involves ensuring continued commitment in-between convening sessions. For there is a crucial window of time at the end of any convening session during which the conversation must be moved into an offering for commitment to whatever project ideas have been generated. Too early and the conversation gets unduly truncated and people feel offended. Too late and the momentum for effecting change on the basis of new ideas is gone. This conversational move must be effected deftly, and by way of general invitation in the form of a "Gift Circle" (Alpha Lo, Charles Eisenstein) or some other like-minded forum.

However the community makes the shift to engagement, the ensuing commitment becomes part of the narrating process that helps to span the gap between sessions. Peter Pula repeatedly emphasizes that this it is the duty of the moderator to ensure these participants meet again, and to help them set the dates. When it is left to them, he says, they invariably fail to re-convene in the future, and key momentum is lost in trying to get them together again. If generativity is to arise, these gaps must be smoothly negotiated, and key narrative work done in the interim that keeps everyone apprised of the status of each other's projects.

Finally, it is essential to note that a moderator needn't be someone hired in, an external consultant of some kind. On the contrary, the moderator is not a person, but a role, and this role can be learned and played by individuals from within the community. In some communities, individuals feel called to fill this role on a regular basis and in others there is an expectation that it rotates among all members. What's key is to have someone who is not caught up in the process itself, and therefore able to give the community their gift of structure and perspective.

> Whole-System Representation

Finally, the group directly participating in the convening-narrative processes must be a reasonable microcosm of the community from which it comes. In particular, discovering ways to build internal and systemic synergy as well as arriving at a state of distributed power in a community can only happen if the key elements of the community system are all present in the process. When elements of a community are missing – regardless of whether those members are considered to be prominent, powerful players, or marginal and disempowered – the dynamics the group ends up embodying will not be in sync with the larger community, and thus the entire effort is likely to fail. The considerations behind the call for whole-system representation in generative community are just as practical as they are moral. In other words, it is not just something communities should do, it's something they must do if they are to be successful.

Whole-system representation in a convening session can be very effective in establishing deeper points of connecting and grounding, even if initially this proves more difficult. Participants from diverse community subgroups often have very different cultural practices, ways of speaking, knowledge about community, and values. All of these differences actually make it more difficult for participants to play their usual roles, and therefore more likely to step into deep connections.

Communities greatly benefit from a body of members that represents the whole community system present in convening-narrating processes when en route to generativity. Similar to the element of critical frequency, there is a sense of "enough" of the system present that should ideally be achieved in order for a generative dynamic to emerge. Too much is rarely the issue.

THE INDIVIDUAL SKILLS OF GENERATIVE COMMUNITIES

Up to this point, the focus has been on a framework and set of practices applicable at the community level. The five conditions, for instance, tell us about how a community is doing in ways that support generativity, and the interplay of convening and narrating are all about nurturing those conditions at the community level.

But this is not the whole story. Fostering generative community also requires the interplay between community practices and individual practices. Generativity, the skillful nurturing of growth and vibrancy in sync with a community and its environment, requires each individual to remain on a path of individual development.

This is abundantly clear when stepping into a generative community. Take St. George's Primary School, in Battersea, London. The moment you walk in the door, you can tell it's a special place. The school has a unique atmosphere of calm, focus, warmth, and determination. This is embodied in the school as a community, in the pedagogy, in their meeting practices, in their school conduct code, and in a range of other community-level practices. But it is also apparent in every individual you meet. The obvious care of the teachers and their drive to support the development of the children in every way. The joy and focus of the administrators to nurture a learning community for their students and teachers. And the exuberance of the students who exude a love of learning and a deep appreciation for the school environment they inhabit.

In other words, generative community is lived in community practices *and* individual skills. Different environments demand different skills. Here we turn to a set of core skills that have demonstrated their value in the kinds of environments essential to generative community. While not intended to be comprehensive, it isolates skills that we are constantly working on and that we see affecting our interactions every day, skills every individual in a generative community needs to develop.

At the same time, it's essential to remember that generative community is an art, not a science, and an evolving art at that. These skills don't represent formulae to apply but elements to "flirt with," to see how much they create the conditions for new possibilities in our own experiences. Nurturing generative community is as much about the acts and intentions of individuals as it is about the work at the community level.

> { *Why vulnerability is key to authentic relationships we don't know. But emotional openness has a way of magically altering the nature of an interaction with others.* }

Vulnerability

The bedrock of generative community is connectedness: people existing in authentic relationships with one another. But authentic relationships don't arise spontaneously. Indeed, as Brené Brown's work has recently highlighted, connection is based on our ability to be vulnerable with others. Vulnerability means opening ourselves up emotionally and personally in ways that seem risky and often inappropriate. In contexts where any signs of weakness, any crack in the wall of rationality and perfection are taken as grounds to attack someone or store their faults for future strikes, then vulnerability seems like a very bad idea. But it is also the one and only key to unlocking authentic relationships.

Why that is remains mysterious. Why it is that being vulnerable is the key to authentic relationships is not something we fully understand. But the experience is clear. Emotional openness has a way of magically altering the nature of an interaction with someone else. What might have begun as posing, or playing expected roles, or straightforward dissemblance can shift in the blink of an eye, when just one person dares to be truly vulnerable. In fact, our experience has shown us that vulnerability is as close as we can get to a silver bullet in fostering authentic relationships because most people seem to automatically respond in kind whenever vulnerability is shown.

How then can we grow into vulnerability? Like learning many other skills, structure can often help us as we begin. Conversation structures are very useful in learning vulnerability. What we have used extensively is a simple "connecting exercise". In this conversation structure groups of 2-4 answer the questions: "Who are you and why are you here?" Each speaker gets four minutes of uninterrupted attention from their group members when they speak and it is very valuable for the other group members to give appreciative feedback after each person has spoken. When one person is finished and the others have given feedback, then the next person can take their turn.

The secrets of this conversation structure are many. The uninterrupted time lets the speaker know that nothing they say will provoke an immediate response. No one is going to contradict them, tell them something they said wasn't clear, or try to turn the conversation in a different direction. The length of time – usually four minutes, although longer can work wonders too – usually allows the speaker to get out some form of mentally prepared content that makes sense as a response to the questions...and then some. The extra time beyond what the person planned to say is when vulnerability often comes into play. Speakers often want to finish there, sensing that they're moving into unknown territory. But the conversation structure dictates that the speaker take all their allotted time, even if they finish in silence. Finally, once the speaker is finished, listeners giving appreciative feedback underscore the safe space created in the connecting exercise, a space for people to show up as whole people, temporarily suspending their roles, their defense mechanisms, and the expectations of others.

Vulnerability can also be practiced in a more informal manner. In conversation with others – both in-person and virtual – we constantly monitor what we feel like saying and what we deem appropriate for the time and context. And the vast majority of us err on side of caution. This is all well and good; it would likely be total chaos if we switched that filtering process off completely. But as we venture farther into vulnerability and learn to see the rich gifts it can bestow upon us and our relationships, simply monitoring that self-censorship is an important first step. Try to watch the filtering in action in your own mind. See what you feel moved to say, what you think suitable for public expression, and what you leave unspoken. As a second step, when you're ready, see if you can find certain unfiltered impulses that you might dare to let through. And then comes the most important part, when you do let those impulses through, when you dare to be more vulnerable than you normally would, what happens? Does chaos ensue? Do you get suddenly attacked? Are you derided or criticized? Or, does something else happen?

In our experience, vulnerability is no silver bullet – but it's pretty darned close! Most often vulnerability leads to a significant deepening of relationships, it leads to unexpected developments in how we are engaged in our communities, how we get our work done, and it lays out a path to greater individual development. It is as if in protecting ourselves from vulnerability, in hiding from the outside, we are also hiding on the inside. Practicing vulnerability, both as a community as in the connecting exercise and as an individual by daring to risk more of ourselves, is the first of the key skills for individuals in generative community.

> Deep listening

Whether we like to admit it or not, few of us are excellent listeners. Our minds are filled with mental chatter, we spend much of our time thinking of what to say next, or we just aren't fully present with whomever is speaking. This is perfectly normal, but it is also a barrier to deep conversations and connection. The soul is shy, as the Quaker philosopher and writer Parker Palmer has written, and it is easily scared off by the ego – one's own or that of others.

It's amazing how rarely deep listening happens. For instance, we have some variant of the connecting exercise described above, in which individuals get at least four minutes of uninterrupted attention from their other group members, hundreds of times. And when people get a chance to reflect on that experience, there is one comment that appears far more often than any other. "I can't remember the last time someone listened to me for four minutes without interrupting."

This is both a sad and an astonishing finding. Whether in personal relationships, at work, or in other communities, we celebrate a culture of speaking, but not of listening. We are judged primarily on how we can respond to a conversation, what we can add, perhaps what question we can ask, but not on how well we can actually listen to what others are saying.

The first result of this is a failure to connect. Like vulnerability, deep listening is a powerful tool in creating a personal connection with someone else. When we speak with one another with our ego seated firmly in our opinions, views, and experiences, we fail to make room for the other. Even when such conversations have a constructive or playful character, as they often can, they still fail to build the depth of connection that happens when we center ourselves less in our ego and give our full attention to someone else.

The other result is that we often fail to hear what the other person is saying. In most communities, a gap of silence longer than two seconds is considered awkward, something to be avoided, a gap to be filled with anything. Practically, this means that we must constantly process what others are saying and prepare our next words. While others are speaking we might be thinking of contrary arguments, or supporting examples from our own experience, or analyzing whether the conversation has gone off topic, or thinking about whether to check our cell phone – in short, a whole litany of things *that are not listening.* And when that becomes our habit – surprise, surprise – we fail to hear what is being spoken.

Deep listening can be practiced in much the same way as practicing vulnerability. The formal path is to use a conversational practice such as the connecting exercise mentioned above, with set times for each speaker. While the speaker's time is running, there are no questions, no interruptions, and no comments. While this doesn't stop the mind from running through its usual patterns, it does make them significantly more apparent and allows the listener to get more comfortable in the space of deep listening. It's amazing how many people feel uncomfortable at first when simply listening.

The informal way to practice deep listening involves first becoming aware of the thoughts that race through the mind while we're ostensibly listening to someone else. Can you hear yourself thinking of responses? Can you sense how you're just waiting for the speaker to finish their sentence so you can unleash your contribution? Can you see how little attention is focused on the speaker? This awareness of our patterns of mind is the first step in deep listening. The second is practice putting them to one side in situations where deep listening seems called for. Once you can see your mind racing, can you let those thoughts float off and refocus your attention on the speaker? Again, and again, and again...

The goal of deep listening is to be wholly and completely with the speaker at every moment. It's a never-ending process to refine this skill. As this skill grows individuals in generative relationships can not only hear a great deal more of what is being said, but the calm openness of deep listening invites the shy soul out of the forest. This practice leads to connection, to healing, and to insight.

> Goodwill

Goodwill is an inner practice that strengthens our intention towards others so that they may experience peace, happiness, health, and loving interactions with others. There's a danger that this can sound rather esoteric or impractical. Nothing could be further from the truth. Generative communities are like gardens gently trying to nurture the abundance that lies dormant in their own seeds. But "gently nurturing a community" is hard work, and one core aspect of that work is being able to see the goodness and potential in each and every person.

In the Buddhist tradition this is called *metta* practice; in the Christian tradition, we find it in many devotions and most clearly in the cult of Mary. No matter the tradition or the particulars of the practice, what all goodwill practices share is first learning to be aware of our inner comportment towards others, and then steer that comportment toward wishes of wellbeing.

This is not about seeing the world through rose-colored glasses. It is not about ignoring what is in front of our eyes. In fact it's not about perception at all. Instead, goodwill practice is a kind of inner "strength training" that we can develop on our own. It is finding that muscle of the soul that has a quality of will towards others and doing the necessary "reps" to build its strength.

Why is strengthening our intention of goodwill to others important in generative relationships? To begin with, comporting ourselves toward others with goodwill allows us to see life and opportunity that may have otherwise remained hidden. Criticism, skepticism, and even bare analysis can often obscure potential that is right in front of our eyes. Thus, with strength of goodwill, we can see the best in others.

But goodwill also has a transformative effect on those with whom we interact. While the exact mechanism by which this operates may remain elusive, the experience is clear. When we have an inner state of goodwill toward others, they can be more vulnerable, they can be more open, and they can find gifts in themselves.

Finally, goodwill is essential to generative relationships because, like deep listening, it is another way to gently place the ego in check. Goodwill is a movement of the self toward the other. In strengthening our capacity to wish others well, we take a step outside the fortress of our self-centeredness and begin to actually feel our connection with those others who constitute our world. It provides an emotional ground for the systemic reality of our everyday lives.

Developing goodwill is most commonly done through a simple contemplative practice. Each person finds a set of phrases that express the felt intention of goodwill towards oneself and others. These are repeated silently for a duration.

Sharon Salzberg, in her book entitled *Loving-kindness*, suggests the following four phrases as a good place to start:

"May I be free from danger."
"May I have mental happiness."
"May I have physical happiness."
"May I have ease of well-being."

Another, slightly simpler variant of the same is:

"May I be peaceful."
"May I be happy."
"May I be healthy"
"May I have ease of well-being."

The exact phrases are unimportant; what is important is that they resonate with you as you develop the intention of goodwill, beginning with yourself as in these examples and then moving on to others one at a time.

"May my wife be peaceful."
"May my wife be happy."
"May my wife be healthy."

"May my wife have ease of well-being."

"May my colleagues be peaceful."
"May my colleagues be happy."
"May my colleagues be healthy."
"May my colleagues have ease of well-being."

As simple as practicing goodwill is, it's not without its difficulties. Many people are turned off by the religious associations of the practice, even if its essence is nothing more than developing an inner comportment towards those around us. Especially in the West, many communities have become allergic to any possibility of mixing our public lives with our personal beliefs. As Alain de Botton has argued, in so doing we have jettisoned many practices that benefit our lives in terms of how we cultivate a sense of community, meaning, perspective, and tenderness. Goodwill practice is one way of relearning those practices.

It is also difficult because, in our rush to get things done, in the crowded schedules of our everyday, taking regular time to develop goodwill towards others seems like a nice extra at best and, to many, a complete waste of time. In fact, generative community is not simply a new practice – it is a new way of being with one another that allows for the emergence of wholeness, synchronicity, care, and innovation. Goodwill practice is one of the foundational tools in learning that way of being.

> Equanimity

Equanimity is neither a common word, nor a common skill. And yet it is essential to nurturing generativity in our relationships and in our communities. The difficult truth is that generativity takes time, often lots of time. In most of our communities, we feel as though we are constantly stuck in the rush of time poverty. Both reason and intuition tell us that longer conversations or more time to reflect would better serve our goals, but we feel the pressure of time pushing us to decide and act quickly.

And this pressure makes itself felt not only in the world of projects, teams, and decisions. The same rush to react takes place in our inner worlds. In meetings and in conversations, something is said and we are quick with an answer, quick with an idea, quick with a criticism. And, of course, our emotional reactions, thoughts, and associations are even faster and more automatic.

Taken together, whether in community situations or in ourselves, our default mode is one of reactivity. We react more or less immediately to whatever happens around us; and this makes a great deal of sense. For goodness sake, our human ancestors would not have made it very far if they'd paused to reflect every time a tiger came leaping out of the grass. Reactivity is a highly useful, habituated skill for mastering everyday life.

But generative community requires a different skill. It requires us to suspend our reactivity through the development of equanimity. In equanimity we first learn to be aware of our perception as well as our automatic categorization and judgment – something we can't shut off unless we go live in a sensory deprivation tank – and then be aware of our impulse to act on that perception, *while doing nothing*. Equanimity is not looking away from what we see. It is not suppressing our emotional reactions. It is not even withholding judgment of our experience. Instead, equanimity is refraining from identifying with our internal reactions and acting on them impulsively.

Of course we are all complicated people. We all have our stresses, our fears, and our "buttons" that trigger reactivity. And far too often these aspects of ourselves become the barriers to deep connection. Either we are too afraid to show them, so we feel unable to tell our whole truth, or we explode into defensiveness, shutting off the lines of open communication.

Equanimity is simply seeing that, between those steps in the chain of experience from perception to reaction, there is a place to pause before we act.

Equanimity is essential in the development of generativity for many reasons. First and foremost, it is a powerful complement to deep listening. Equanimity allows us to hear our own judgments and thoughts, and suspend them while we stay with the speaker. We temper our need to answer too quickly. As we strengthen this muscle of inner balance, we can be more fully present with the other; a strength of presence that has transformative effects.

In truth, practicing equanimity is not terribly easy. It takes patience itself! One way is to stay present with the body, trying to notice any sensations that occur, positive, negative, and neutral. Tension, pain, relaxation, pleasure, cold, pressure, etc. In that noticing you create a small separation, a small gap in which equanimity can grow. Noticing is the way to break the chain of reactivity.

The same applies to the workings of our thoughts, emotions, and impulses to act. While noticing *these* experiences as they happen is even more difficult than doing so for the body, as we learn to observe them – simple non-analytic, non-judgmental observation – we simultaneously build the muscle of equanimity. We strengthen our ability to remain aware of the present without taking the step into action.

> A never-ending process

Vulnerability, deep listening, goodwill, and equanimity are four fundamental skills individuals can develop to support generativity. We could have added many more – sensing, compassion, and contextualizing come to mind – but the point is not to be comprehensive. The point is that generativity is about both the community and the individual. Nurturing the conditions of generative community requires that communities use the supporting practices of convening and narrating just as much as it requires individuals within those communities to attend to their own individual skills. Each of us is different and comes with different histories and aptitudes, all of which will impact how quickly or thoroughly we can develop these individual skills. These four skills are a worthy place to begin this never-ending process.

MEASURING GENERATIVITY

The measures of success within generative communities may be qualitative, but they are not mysterious. The goal of nurturing generative community is focused on the power of self-efficacy and engagement. The community cycle delivers concrete indices that can be used to assess the state and growth of individual communities.

Connection

> Do community members know one another?
> Are trust and openness developed in the community?
> Is there a good map of community members and assets?
> Is it easy to find others who want to co-create?

Grounding

> Do community members feel grounded in shared values and a common identity?
> Is the purpose of the community a common topic in discussion?
> Are there regular practices of reflection upon values and goals?

Informing

> Is there an evolving, nuanced understanding of the state of the community?
> Are there effective ways to share learning in the community?
> Is there a common (virtual) space for building community knowledge and learning more about the community?

Discussing

> Are there inclusive, collaborative, and constructive discussions to co-create the desired future of the community?
> Are all relevant stakeholders regularly present for community discussion?
> Do community discussions build effectively on one another, creating greater depth and breadth of understanding?

Engaging

> Do community members know how to get involved in the current prototyping in the community?
> Do community members feel self-empowered to affect the course of their community?
> Are community members motivated to engage with their community?

It seems that the best way to use these measures is through a combination of formal surveys taken at set points in a project and informal talks with community members. Using these formal and informal feedback loops will (1) ensure that we stay on-target, learning where our efforts can be adjusted and (2) provide us with "evidence" to demonstrate to others the efficacy of what we're doing.

INSPIRATION & INFLUENCES

This text was not cut from whole cloth. Riffing on but one influence, we could say that the three of us wrote this book together, and since each of us was several, there was already quite a crowd.

> A book has neither object nor subject; it is made of variously formed matters, and very different dates and speeds. To attribute the book to a subject is to overlook this working of matters, and the exteriority of their relations. It is to fabricate a beneficent God to explain geological movements. In a book, as in all things, there are lines of articulation or segmentarity, strata and territories; but also lines of flight, movements of deterritorialization and destratification.

(Deleuze and Guattari, A Thousand Plateaus, 3-4:1987)

Of course, naming each influence, every person, idea, and experience that flows through us into this text, would be an impossible and silly task. And yet the desire to look back and point to those influences is clearly present. Like the great trading nodes of history – Odessa, Baghdad, Constantinople – we have set out to combine these influences in a way both unique and exciting, while still celebrating the riches that have been delivered from afar.

> Generative design

Otto Scharmer

Theory U: leading from the future as it emerges (Berrett-Koehler, 2009)

Leading from the emerging future: from ego-system to eco-system economies (Berrett-Koehler, 2013) [with Katrin Kaufer]

John McKnight

The Abundant Community: awakening the power of families and neighborhoods (Berrett-Koehler, 2012) [with Peter Block]

Peggy Holman

The Change Handbook: the definitive resource on today's best methods for engaging whole systems (Berrett-Koehler, 2007) [with Devane and Cady]

Engaging Emergence: turning upheaval into opportunity (Berrett-Koehler, 2010)

Peter Block

Community: the structure of belonging (Berrett-Koehler, 2009)

The Answer to How is Yes: acting on what matters (Berrett-Koehler, 2003)

C. Scott Peck

The Road Less Travelled (Simon and Schuster, 1978)

The Different Drum: community making and peace (Touchstone, 1987)

David Bohm

On Dialogue (Routledge, 1996)

Peter Pula

Axiom News, Peterborough, Canada (www.axiomnews.com)

> Systems thinking

Donella Meadows

Thinking in Systems: a primer (Chelsea Green Publishing, 2008)

Jamshid Gharajedaghi

Systems Thinking: managing chaos and complexity (Morgan Kaufmann, 2011)

Peter Senge

Presence: human purpose and the field of the future (SoL, 2004) [with Otto Scharmer, Joseph Jaworski, and Betty Sue Flowers]

Gregory Bateson

Steps to an Ecology of Mind (Jason Aronson, 1987)

Jay Forrester

Industrial Dynamics (MIT Press, 1963)

> Philosophy of living systems/patterns

Christopher Alexander

A Pattern Language: towns, buildings, construction (Oxford University Press, 1977)

The Nature of Order, Books 1-4 (Center for Environmental Studies, 2002-2003)

Fritjof Capra

The Tao of Physics: an exploration of the parallels between modern physics and eastern mysticism (Shambhala Publications, 1975)

The Systems View of Life: a unifying vision (Cambridge University Press, 2014) [with Pier Luigi Luisi]

Duane Elgin

The Living Universe (Berrett-Koehler Press, 2009)

Humberto Maturana

The Origin of Humanness in the Biology of Love (Imprint Academic, 2009) [with Gerda Verden-Zöller]

The Tree of Knowledge: the biological roots of human understanding (Shambhala Publications, 1987) [with Francisco Varela]

Joanna Macy

Coming Back to Life (new society publishers, 2014)& Molly Brown

Fréderic Laloux

Reinventing Organizations: a guide to creating organizations inspired by the next stage of human consciousness (Nelson Parker, 2015)

Thomas Berry

The Great Work: our way into the future (Bell Tower, 1990)

> Power of narrative

Walter Brueggemann

The Prophetic Imagination (Canterbury Press, 1978)

David Abram

The Spell of the Sensuous: perception and language in a more-than-human world (Vintage Books, 1997)

Stephen Denning

The Leader's Guide to Storytelling: mastering the art and discipline of business narrative (Jossey-Bass, 2011)

Wendell Berry

"Solving for Pattern", Chapter 9 in *The Gift of Good Land: Further Essays Cultural & Agricultural* (North Point Press, 1981)

David Cooperrider

Appreciative inquiry: a positive revolution in change (Berrett-Koehler, 2005) [with Diana Whitney]

> Power of vulnerability and authenticity

Parker Palmer

A Hidden Wholeness: the journey toward an undivided life (Jossey-Bass, 2004)

Healing the Heart of Democracy: the courage to create a politics worthy of the human spirit (Jossey-Bass, 2011)

Judy Cannato

Field of Compassion: how the new cosmology is transforming spiritual life (Sorin Book, 2010)

Brené Brown

Daring Greatly: how the courage to be vulnerable transforms the way we live, love, parent and lead (Avery Publishing, 2012)

Margaret Wheatley

Leadership and the New Science: discovering order in a chaotic world (Berrett-Koehler, 2006)

Turning to One Another: simple conversations to restore hope to the future (Berrett-Koehler, 2009)

Richard Rohr

Immortal Diamond: searching for our true self (SPCK Publishing, 2013)

Marshall Rosenberg

Nonviolent Communication: a language of life (Puddle Dancer Press, 2003)

> Miscellaneous

Alain de Botton

Religion for Atheists: a non-believer's guide to the uses of religion (Hamish Hamilton, 2012)
The News: a user's manual (Hamish Hamilton, 2014)

Yochai Benkler

The Wealth of Networks: how social production transforms markets and freedom (Yale University Press, 2006)

Robert D. Putnam

Better together: restoring the American community (Simon & Schuster, 2003). [with Lewis Feldstein]

Hartmut Rosa

Resonanz: eine Soziologie der Weltbeziehung (Suhrkamp, 2016)

Sharon Salzberg

Lovingkindness: the revolutionary art of happiness (Shambhala, 1995)

Saint George's Church of England Primary School

http://www.st-georges.wandsworth.sch.uk/
https://vimeo.com/178801747

CONCLUSION

What we are engaging in when we nurture generative communities is something both very ancient and something very new. It is ancient in that we are recovering the qualities and practices of self-healing and self-organization that communities have known for centuries. It is safe to say that most communities for most of human history have developed their own, unique cultural practices for sustaining connections with one another, for grounding themselves in their identity and values, for gaining knowledge about the state of their world, for deciding what future they want to create, and for making that shared vision a reality.

The work of building generative community is also new, because we as a people of the Earth have created new social pathologies – size, speed, alienation, and rationalization – for which we must now seek healing. Nurturing generative community seeks to honor both the wisdom our communities have to create their own abundance and the reality of where they stand in the early 21st century. We – the contributors to this snapshot – share the conviction that nurturing communities to live joyfully in this cycle of connecting, grounding, informing, discussing and engaging is one key to that healing.

We feel it would be remiss to imply that this is easy work. It is not. The mindset that undergirds the interpersonal, organizational, and social structures we are seeking to counterbalance is based in fear, in the need for security, in the desire to control. It is a powerful mindset. Love does not always win.

Hope does not spring eternal. Our very success as a species is due in large part to these "baser" tendencies to avoid danger at all cost, to erect powerful structures of domination; to hoard, control, and attack.

Becoming generative individuals and nurturing generative communities requires us to see the mindset of fear, security, and control as a tool fit for some occasions, but not all. This is so very difficult because it is a default mindset, one to which we return whenever the going gets tough, whenever we're tired or scared or simply unsure of how to proceed. And it is the default way of structuring most schools, organizations, companies, and societies. For most, fear and control are the last things to go, while connection and presence are the first.

Many of our mentors over the years have noted, as we have, that you can't do this work with everyone. Generative, resonant relationships require a level of openness, presence, vulnerability, and will that many do not yet embody. The dance of generativity cannot happen without them. Our advice: don't even try. Trying to reform people, communities, or institutions that are squarely operating out of the mindset of fear, security, and control is a waste of time. Like pouring scarce water on seeds that will never sprout, it is a waste that benefits no one while depriving others who could urgently use support.

We say this not to discourage, and certainly not from a spirit of pessimism. Quite to the contrary. Perhaps our biggest challenge in this work, as in life, is learning how to love well. Love not as a feeling, nor as an intention, but as a practice. One which requires our full attention. We are firmly convinced that nurturing generative communities is at the core of practicing love in the world, of bringing us into resonance with ourselves, with each other, and with the world. We need simply know where to dance and with whom.

Finally, we want it to be clear that we do not intend *The Way of Generativity* to stand as an intellectual monolith, as a comprehensive explication of the what, why, and how of generativity in communities. We hope that the concepts and language developed here are of use in creating a community of practice, so that individuals and groups may look up from the page with a renewed sense of clarity and will in living its values. And we hope it can be a beacon and inspiration to unsure souls that they too may venture forth to lands their hearts are already urging them to discover.

GENERATIVE COSMOLOGY, AND WHY IT MATTERS

Our dominant worldview, our intellectual thought processes, and our institutions were created by men who wanted neat, tidy, and repeatable processes, mostly for material gain, in a clockwork universe.

We have known for some time that the universe is mysterious, full of emerging possibilities and probabilities, but our thought processes, language, and social structures do not reflect our knowledge of the world, or this cosmology.

We cannot build joyful, creative, inclusive, and sustainable societies without acknowledging the intentional and relational nature of the universe. It is, in the words of Sister Ilia Delio, an "open world of change and play." In our modern world, the innocence and wonder of a child has been largely replaced by hard reason and a need for intensive scientific validation of "reality."

> What is cosmology and why does it matter?

Cosmology constitutes our worldview, our best reflection of the nature of the universe and our role in it. Cosmology is important not for a correct intellectual view, not about "getting it right." Instead, cosmology, consciously used, can give us permission to trust our intuition, especially when verging on a future unknown.

For us, cosmology, convening, and generative narratives are all about enabling a community to be in a flow-state of learning, able to sense and take the next best step.

Throughout human history, questions about the origin and nature of the universe have been front and center. Stories and songs told of its birth. Works of art embodied a shared cosmological understanding. Rituals, feasts, and harvests took part in the universe's cycles, and each person carried with him or her a tacit understanding that informed their decisions.

Today, the cosmology most of us are familiar with is that of the stars. In recent centuries, cosmology has primarily addressed celestial bodies, as astronomers and physicists speculate about the origins of the universe. It might pique our interest to read in *Scientific American* about a new theory of the expanding universe or give us slight pangs of fear pondering when the Great Crunch might happen, but cosmology today has little to do with our everyday lives.

That is a shame, because as we sink further into the dominant clockwork cosmology – a lifeless, godless, mechanical apparatus that is understandable, divisible, and controllable in every way – it becomes harder to see how it rules our thinking, our decisions, and our society. This is especially ironic considering that the field of physics, originally its forbearer, has long since moved beyond it. A joke between modern-day physics majors is that "engineers are physicists who don't like quantum." But we are stuck with the residue of an antiquated paradigm of classical physics.

It hasn't always been this way.

Before cosmology became the subject solely of astrophysics, the structure and dynamics of the universe were central and important topics throughout discussions both learned and everyday. Even if we limit our focus to the West, we can see how radical the changes and clashes have been, from the Biblical cosmology of God creating heaven and earth to the Atomist cosmology of Epicurus consisting of nothing more than atoms and emptiness in a godless universe. Or the great shifts from the medieval geocentric universe to the revolution of Copernicus and on to Newton's discovery of gravity, Einstein's relativity, and beyond.

In one sense, each of these shifts was little more than a new theory backed up by some reasoning, evidence, or belief. Mere equations on a page. But in another, very real sense, these shifts in cosmology completely changed the

92

world. Our cosmologies matter deeply because they are the unseen lenses through which we perceive and understand the world. They form our experience of the world, they structure our understanding, and they guide our decisions.

The pre-Socratic philosopher Epicurus (341-270 BC), for instance, whose cosmology included neither gods nor an afterlife, left the bustle of Athens and bought a little farm on the edge of the city where he lived with friends enjoying the simple pleasures of food, companionship, and conversation. Martin Luther, in contrast, devoted his life and study to a radically different cosmology – a direct relationship between God and servant – that led him to battle the Catholic Church his entire life and eventually cost him excommunication. These were lives lived, decisions made, because of the cosmology each carried.

Today is no different. We each live our lives filtering experience, interpreting the world, and making choices based on our own particular cosmology, our own implicit understanding of the structure and dynamics of the universe. That's why this is not a lofty academic discussion or a diversion into theory. Cosmology is the basis for how we live our lives. That's why we think it crucial to recognize the cosmology dominant today, as well as outline a more accurate one that we find is also more life-giving and conducive to generating vibrant communities.

> The Eternal Dance

We can all sense when things go too far one way or the other. When one is too pumped up, when one is *too* relaxed, when one is giving too much or too little. Ueli Steck, the famous Swiss speed-climber, who recently climbed the North Face of the Eiger in less than half the time it had ever been climbed in before, said, "If I'm starting to get excited, to twitch, to feel like a god, I back off that – if I'm starting to get lax, and my thoughts wander, or I get worried about something else, something *after* my climb, I go faster – somewhere, amidst that, I climb."

Premise #1: The universe thrives in the dance between many opposites.

The cosmology underpinning our community-building work is in many ways similar to this description by Steck. Over the years we have discovered and wrestled with a growing number of opposites, all of which animate the work.

To take just one pair – narrating and convening – communities must convene to connect, to share their progress, and check in on their story, but they must not convene too much lest they interrupt each other's work or get lost in the simple joy of companionship. Conversely, communities must narrate, share what is happening and what needs to happen. But, again if they do that for too long without gathering together they will risk falling out of touch, coming unmoored, and deviating from the communal purpose already built. We must make, and we must share. Vibrant growth is found in the dance between these activities. And in order to develop shared understanding and collective intelligence, that dance is best done in community.

micro	macro
narrating	convening
heart	mind
spirituality	science
awe	understanding
self	other
being	doing
organism	niche

Premise #2: The universe doesn't rest in balance; it rides in the tension.

When facing these opposites, two tempting, but dangerous responses suggest themselves. The most common involves recognizing a point of long-standing imbalance, a personal, institutional, or structural habit that sways to one extreme or the other, and then simply jumping to the other extreme. Perhaps a school community sees how giving grades has led to an overemphasis on performance, to stress and competition. So how might they react? Get rid of grades entirely. Hierarchy ruining innovation at a company? Fire the managers! In almost all cases, this reaction merely leads to a new imbalance as the opposing extreme takes the throne.

There's a second reaction that is somewhat harder to see: looking for the perfect "balance" between the poles. This other tendency recognizes the productive value of both extremes and then seeks to find a static balance, a resting point from which to base optimal growth. The problem with this search for balance is that life doesn't sit still. A point of seeming balance today will be suddenly off-kilter as the world with which we interact changes, as it always does. And thus, such a search often yields inadequate compromises, at best, which are quickly outdated and dissatisfying to all parties.

Our work and play have revealed the importance of many opposites. One core realization in generative communities is their need for both convening and narration. Communities, we have learned, need times of both activity and celebration. It requires both the work of the mind and the labor of the heart. But these opposites do not allow of any "balance" because there is no static point of perfection we are aiming for. The cosmology out of which generative communities emerge encounters a universe replete with these opposites in an eternal dance.

Consider the interchange of science and religion, for instance, as addressed extensively in the works of the Franciscan friar Richard Rohr and Sister Ilia Delio. Science, both note, is involved with the language of inference; it conducts observations and draws inferences therefrom that are in turn codified into theories. Religion, by contrast, is concerned with building a person's sense of awe of the rhythms of the cosmos. It is concerned with scope, with appreciation, with empathetic union with the more-than-human. How are we to comport ourselves toward a universe that presents itself in such disparate modes? What are we to do with this seeming clash between science and religion?

We are suggesting that the answer is neither in choosing one or the other, nor is it in finding an ideal balance between them. Instead, these two perspectives are highly compatible in a dialectical manner, entering into a dance between them that never ceases. If we become overly scientific, we become too concerned with extracting theories from the cosmos, and lose our bearing on which theories will be useful and assist us. If we become too religious, we run the risk of what Hermann Hesse called lapsing into the "mystical," simply dissolving into a spellbound state of appreciation. While beautiful, it is also impotent.

The importance of this perspective lies in its synchrony with the theme of "never stopping."

This learning never stops because, again, there is no static balancing point to be reached, after which we simply lean back into an ether of Nirvana. You can always home further in on the forbidden middle, even as gusts of wind suddenly throw the teeter-totter one way or the other.

The celebrated playwright Sam Shepard once said, "right smack in the middle of a contradiction, that's where I want to be. That's where the heat is." And that's also where we find generative community.

Anyone with a calculator can turn conventional truths. We are in deeper waters, and thus we suggest a dialectical path forward. For that is how we can help communities discover what they already always knew, what they readily discover in the time-space of connection and reflection. Generative communities thrive on this playful interchange between participants, between participants and community, and between community and its larger environment. The biologist Humberto Maturana calls this the "co-evolution of organism and niche," in that both design each other as they develop in concert. Autopoeisis, or self-creation – the driving mechanism of all living systems. We can learn to live within the core of this driving force.

> Living systems

> We have sought for firm ground and found none. The deeper we penetrate, the more restless becomes the universe; all is rushing about and vibrating in a wild dance.

Max Born, *The Restless Universe* 1936, 277

Premise #3: Cosmologies should be chosen on the basis of both accuracy and utility.

Choosing a more refined cosmology means dealing with one further set of opposites: accuracy versus utility. Every cosmology is a theory of how the universe works. We, as limited perceivers easily prone to information overload, need these theories, these simplified models of the world in order to process the flood our senses are presented with. We need them to make any decision at all. Cosmologies arise to help us deal with the unfathomable diversity of the universe.

It shouldn't surprise us, though, that useful cosmologies approximate the infinite diversity of the universe in ways that also correspond – more or less –

to its actual behavior. Even a cosmology such as the geocentric model of ancient European and Islamic astronomers got right that the sun, planets, stars, and Earth were all separate bodies orbiting around one another in a regular fashion. Yes, they erred in placing the Earth at the middle of this system. But in many ways the cosmology was both useful and accurate as demonstrated by its dominance for more than a millennium.

Perhaps no better example of this interplay between the accuracy and utility of cosmologies can be found than that of the well-known wave-particle duality observed at the subatomic level. The experimental details and interpretations thereof are extraordinarily complex and, indeed, conflicted up to this very day. What is clear, however, is that sometimes when the universe is observed at the microscopic level it behaves as if made up of probability waves, while at other times it behaves as if made up of discrete particles. Thus, two very different and (likely) incompatible cosmologies remain both accurate and useful in different settings.

We are thus faced with the fact that there is no single cosmology that can fulfill all our demands. All cosmologies possess some measure of accuracy and utility, otherwise they would have fallen victim to the throes of cultural evolution. Our question is, thus, more nuanced: which cosmology is appropriate for us right now? Which cosmology opens up the greatest potential for life and emergence? The first part of the answer: not the mechanical cosmology.

Premise #4: The mechanical cosmology has outlived its utility.

The dominant cosmology of the 20th century – and indeed since Newton and Descartes (17th c.), if not Galileo and Copernicus (15th/16th c.) – saw the universe as a machine. According to this cosmology, everything in the universe, from billiard balls and apples to plants and humans, is composed exclusively of discrete parts that interact with one another following a single set of causal and deterministic laws. This is the world of Newtonian physics that has colored the views of nearly everyone with a Western education and cultural upbringing.

What began as an approach to understanding physical bodies on Earth and in the heavens – where this kind of mechanical cosmology does an admirable job of describing and predicting the movement of matter – was then zealously applied to other fields in the hard sciences: biology, physiology, chemistry, evolution, and genetics. Indeed, its success in providing neat and elegant descriptions in these burgeoning sciences led to its further application in philosophy, sociology, economics, management theory, public schooling, and even political theory, where its success was harder to gauge.

In short, this mechanical cosmology has been wildly easy to import and apply, in some way to our great benefit. The ubiquity of public schooling, the rise in economic standards, the progress of medicine, the explosion of technology and productivity – to name but a few – all owe their success to the methodical application of a mechanical cosmology to those domains. But just because a hammer is good for breaking stones, doesn't mean it's good for breaking eggs.

We sense the need to supersede this mechanical cosmology for many reasons. But to start with, it's causing problems.

These problems are everywhere to be found. Health care service is suffering as the relationships between doctor and patient are broken down and managed like a well-tuned, complicated machine, resulting in more data, more bureaucracy, and less real care. Schooling is suffering from these same mechanized, best-practices approaches destroying the relationships between teacher and pupil; stripping teachers of their agency and turning students into outcomes, not people. And the economy is suffering as we instrumentalize the very people for whom it is meant to work and orient our decisions toward GDP or profit or productivity.

And this realization is not new. More than a century ago, the English art critic and essayist John Ruskin wrote, in "The Roots of Honour," that in over-mechanizing the process, you conflate means and ends. The means are the machines, the output, and the money. The ends are people and their development and the generation of real works, both artistic and intellectual. If the means become overly valued, at the expense of the ends, a dehumanization takes place as people become machines in a great mechanized process. Yet, this is exactly what has happened again and again as the mechanical cosmology has been applied to ever more fields of Western life.

Premise #5: Living systems are interconnected wholes. No "part" has either an existence or function separate from the whole.

In all of these cases and many, many more the mechanical cosmology is guilty of breaking down a complex system, be it the health of an individual, the learning process of a child, or the fulfilling work-life of our societies, into constituent parts, tearing them out of the relationships that make them who and what they are, and then trying to optimize each part individually. Once each part is optimized, through standards, best practices, command, and control, then – so the thinking goes – the whole will thrive as well.

Unfortunately, this is bad thinking.

It's bad thinking because in living systems no part stands in isolation from any other. Change the behavior of one aspect of a system and you change the dynamics of it as a whole. Optimization of parts, even when it might seem to work, fails to take into account this fundamentally systemic, relationship-based nature of people, groups, organizations, and communities.

Of course, it might look like it's working. Focusing on individual parts often creates short-term improvements in key measures, only to have negative effects rebound farther down the line. Ultimately this leaves the system in a worse place than where it started. For instance, the recent heightened focus in American education on test scores has, in many cases, led to classroom practices that have indeed boosted scores – by teaching to the test, cutting extracurricular activities, and learning the "tricks" of test taking.

At the same time, however, this focus on one particular "part" of education – test scores – has brought with it a decline in real understanding of the subject matter, increased stress for the pupils, and a loss of passion among teaching staff as they themselves become factory supervisors. In failing to see the entire system of a school – students, teachers, administrators, parents, and beyond – the focus on an individual part has ignored the dynamics and feedback loops in which that part is enmeshed, leading to a gradual undermining of the policy's efficacy.

By contrast – and this is *essential* to understand – when real systemic changes are put into effect, the system often performs worse for a time before arcing into a course of sustained improvement. To take a further school example, when standards obsessions are suddenly dropped and mentorships focusing on the cultivation of students' abilities are put in place, students are often momentarily disoriented and perform *worse* on standardized tests. With time, however, they learn how to apply their own unique learnings *to* the test and their scores become better than they ever were.

Premise #6: Properties in livings systems emerge from the interactions of the whole, not individual parts.

The real cosmological revolution in living systems is the shift of focus from parts to the whole. This is a real departure from the mechanical cosmology, where the behavior and properties of a whole are seen to be caused by individual parts. The heat of a combustion engine, for example, is caused by the release of energy in the explosion within each piston. This much is true – indeed, the mechanical cosmology is generally useful when applied to car engines. But this method of identifying the source of heat in an engine causes major problems when applied to a range of other phenomena such as ecosystems, weather, and communities, which are not so easily isolable.

Studying these phenomena benefits from taking a different view, a living-systems view, because their behaviors and properties cannot be understood by inspecting individual parts but by understanding the emergent interactions between their parts. Think of a strained marriage. Both parties experience coolness from one another, minor insensitivities are blown out of proportion, and no one is happy. A marriage, too, is a living system and thus the solution is not to separate the two, fix their "problems" and put the marriage back together. That's because the properties of the marriage – in this case, lacking warmth, sensitivity, and happiness – are not produced by the parts but by the interaction of the parts. What's easy to see in a relationship of two people, at least from the outside, is the same as in a larger school community or geographic community. The very properties that we would like to influence – performance, test scores, productivity, and engagement – are not those of individual parts but of the interactions between the parts that make up the whole.

These are called emergent properties. Emergent properties force a shift of perspective from the reductionist, mechanical view towards the holistic, systemic viewpoint. When this occurs, one does not see static objects bouncing off one another but dynamic processes manifesting in temporary structures, often unexpectedly. As the chemist Ilya Prigogene once said, "one cannot understand emergent properties by taking apart the system. The system must be looked at as a *whole.*"

This, in turn, leads us to the last salient aspect of living systems we want to highlight here: nonlinear causality.

Premise #7: With the mechanical cosmology also goes mechanical causality. Causality in living systems is nonlinear.

The stark differences between the notions of causality in the mechanical cosmology and the living-systems cosmology could hardly be greater. Take poverty in a neighborhood, for example. In the mechanical view, poverty is an attribute of individual families or people. Poverty can thus be defined as the relative lack of wealth and income of these people. And given this view, the solution is obvious: give money to those who are poor. Welfare, social benefits, and negative income taxes are all attempts to solve the problem of poverty with a mechanical view. The real problem is that, however necessary such programs are to reduce the suffering of the members of our communities, they don't solve much in the long-run.

From the living-systems viewpoint, poverty is not an attribute of a person – there are no "poor people" – rather poverty is the emergent property of a system expressed in part by the relative lack of wealth and income of some community members. Poverty, from this viewpoint, is not a fixed state, but an ongoing process. It is a verb, not a noun. And poverty is a process of the system as a whole, not only those who manifest the symptoms. Thus a living-systems approach would look not for "fixes," but for practices that can lead to improved dynamics within the community. And it would look at the entire system of these dynamics in order to identify the most likely leverage points for nudging the system as a whole toward greater health.

None of this thinking is particularly new. Already in the 1960s, Jay Forrester, a widely celebrated inventor at MIT, studied a series of low-income communities who seemed to be sinking further into poverty. All attempts to provide them with better housing, by constructing new housing projects, for instance, only worsened the situation. For such efforts only brought more people to the area and increased the number of those who were suffering. To find more systemic solutions to the situation, Jay began creating system-dynamics models, which, in their qualitative form, are called 'systems maps.' Through this work, Jay found that the systemic problem lay not in the availability of living quarters, but in the isolation of the community itself. There was no public transit nearby. No highways. No way for this residential community to interact with the larger urban system and provide its citizens with work. Thus, Jay advocated for road building and the extension of public transit, and once this was granted, members of the community began entering the workforce, and the system began to revive itself.

What we see in these examples is that our understanding of causality itself – how it is that things happen – is very different in the mechanical cosmology than in that of living systems. In the mechanical cosmology, separate objects directly influence others with which they come in direct contact. But living systems are different. They are different because there are no separate objects. It no longer makes sense to speak of individual parts, only processes interacting with one another. What's more, because every living system contains several of these processes interacting, every nudge to one process necessarily influences all others. This means a fundamental change in how we nurture living systems.

Premise #8: Living systems are complex, but not incomprehensible.

One common response to seeing communities and other phenomena as living systems is a growing frustration that comes from the complexity they display. As the neat, separate parts of an orderly mechanical system fade away and are replaced by dynamics, flows, and emergent properties, many fight the urge to throw in the towel. This is a good fight to have, for living systems are complex, but not incomprehensible. And the most common way to comprehend them is by developing systems maps.

Systems maps do not look like the static blueprints of a building. Systems maps represent three aspects of a system: (1) the main components, (2) their relative influence, and (3) the interactions in between. Not only do systems maps represent dynamic systems, but they themselves also change over time, as the systems they represent continue to evolve their structure over time amidst environmental changes. This is what renders them non-mechanical, but living. The maps only represent the system at one point in time, and often contain within them the seeds of their future versions.

Systems maps make it possible to see the complex whole at that instant, to see the core dynamics of the system itself. This is the first benefit of systems mapping: it makes the complexity manageable. Every system – a community or an ecosystem, for example – is in fact incomprehensibly complex. An almost uncountable number of factors are ceaselessly interacting with one another in both regular and irregular ways. But a systems map, by highlighting the most salient components and dynamics of their interrelations, makes it increasingly possible to see the system as a whole and to begin sensing the connections between the many dynamics. Like any other map, its purpose is not to represent reality per se, but to allow us to find our way. A systems map is a tool to aid us in seeing. We need all the help we can get.

Of course the novice vegetable gardener is overwhelmed with all the factors before him or her: water, sunlight, companion plants, insects, animals, soil temperature, nutrients, and so on. But over the years, the gardener learns to both intuitively sense and rationally understand how the garden as a living system works, how the numerous dynamics interact. With time, the garden begins to flourish.

Beyond growing to sense and understand a system, systems maps also answer the more important question: *where do I start?* The good news is that there's no wrong answer to this.

Because of the interrelations between all the dynamics that make up a system, nurturing the health of one nurtures the health of all others (or at least, do no harm). If we find a school community, for instance, in which relationships are poorly established, there is little shared understanding, discussions are not constructive, and behavior is based on old patterns, then addressing any of these would be of benefit to the whole. Why? Because what is being "addressed" is not a part extracted from the whole, but a dynamic integrally connected to the whole.

It's almost as if the universe has given us that good with the bad. Yes, mechanical systems are easy to understand, but almost any change one makes to an individual part is likely to have negative unintended consequences. And the opposite is true as well. Yes, living systems are extraordinarily complex and hard to grasp, but almost any change one makes is likely to have a positive consequence. This is the essential difference between the mechanical, symptomatic approach and the holistic, systems approach. The latter always looks for the next step toward greater wholeness. The particularities are less important than the attention to the whole.

The path through the cosmology supporting generative communities has been from less to greater complexity. We began with the observation that riding the tension between many opposites leads to greater learning and growth. From that eternal dance we then moved on to seeing the faults of the mechanical cosmology and the utility of seeing through the lens of living systems, replete with emergent properties, nonlinear causality, and systems maps. We believe all this to be necessary and good, for this cosmological perspective puts us in a place of greater joy, finer sensitivity, and deeper understanding.

But even this is not the whole picture, for at the horizon of this understanding is something just as necessary, something less clear, something more wonderful.

> Cosmic awe

> The five colors blind the eye.
> The five tones deafen the ear.
> The five flavors dull the taste.
> Racing and hunting madden the mind.
> Precious things lead us astray.
> Therefore the wise are guided by what they feel and not what they see,
> Letting go of that and choosing this.

Lao Tsu, *Tao Te Ching*, verse 12

The Buddha once said to one his disciples, "you are in danger of being too clever." Analysis, understanding, knowledge – all these can take us a great distance. But when you overanalyze, when you get cozy in an understanding, or when you become sure of your knowledge, you begin to destroy the wonder that is at the heart of the cosmos and our unfolding role within it, and you become detached from our ability to sense with more than the mind alone.

Of course the Buddha wasn't against making distinctions or carrying on arguments. The stories that recount his teaching life are full of lists, analyses, and other philosophical finery. The mechanical, distinction-making perspective – binaries; *this* or *that* – is useful for tool-making. But it is *not* sufficient for directly sensing the impossible complexity (and beautiful simplicity) of the universe as it modulates through us.

As we go deeper and deeper into these intricate analytical understandings, penetrating the likes of causality, living systems, and dialectical frameworks, we feel, quite properly, after a time, that we do not understand anything at all. This is good. Recall the Max Born quote: "The deeper we penetrate, the more restless becomes the universe; all is rushing about and vibrating in a wild dance." There comes a point when you have to throw up your arms and say, who knows? That is what we like to think of as 'reasoned ignorance.' It came on the heels of a good effort, and it is earned.

This exhaustion can make for the beginning of the productive side of this awe.

Every dive into the depths of knowledge leads to greater understanding. However, it's always necessary to resurface and transform that knowledge into wiser action. And this wiser action cannot rest solely on that which the mind alone sees. It must also honor other forms of wisdom: the wisdom of intuition, the wisdom of our communities, the wisdom of the heart.

Cosmic awe is understanding the limits of our knowledge and trusting that these other forms of wisdom are just as valid and necessary paths to greater generativity in a community.

> Like our ancestors, we bow to the vastness of the undertaking, to the beauty that hides in the unknown, beckoning us. It is awe that fuels us [...]. Awe is the bridge between our past and our present, taking us forward into the future as we keep on searching.

> Marcelo Gleiser, *The Island of Knowledge*, 2014: 283

> The Effect on Us

This cosmological stance has done something with us. Not by force, not by duty – seeing the world in this way has awakened in us one final dance of opposites between "self" and "other". Seeing the world as a set of living systems dissolves the isolation of the ego. Gradually, egocentric behavior makes less sense and, like a sunflower turning toward the sun, an orientation towards nurturing oneself, others, and community alike becomes a source of interest and joy for both the individual and the community itself.

Ultimately, cosmology is important not for a correct intellectual view. It's not about "getting it right." Instead, cosmology, consciously used, can give us permission to trust our cells, to make imagination reality. Most importantly, for us, cosmology, convening, and generative narratives are all about enabling a community to be in a flow-state of learning, able to sense and take the next step.

SUMMARY

Individuals in communities of all kinds are seeking new ways of being and being together. Whether in schools, teams, large organizations, or municipalities – all of which we see as communities – we find a growing sense of unease. Our ways may have been adequate in the 20th century, but not anymore. The question is: how can a new way of being allow us to act differently?

That is our guiding question. And we think there are some good answers.

As the structures and dynamics of the communities forged in the 20th century begin to cause more struggle, the seeds of a new era are germinating, sprouting, and even flourishing in small beds around the globe. From a spiritual center in Iowa to a state ministry in Austria, from an elementary school in London to a city in Ontario, we have witnessed new ways of being in community that have a great deal to teach us all.

We call this the way of generativity. Generative individuals in generative communities embody a way of being that nurtures individuals, groups, and their environment to grow into deep resonance with one another. Because individuals, groups, and their environments are in deep connection with one another, they develop true care. Because they care, they support each other in the development of their highest potential. Because they support their mutual development, they flourish.

Like starting a new garden, preparing the soil takes time and effort. Tending new plants requires attention and patience; the true beauty and resilience of a garden takes years to develop. So too with generativity. Generativity takes time, effort, attention, and patience. Our anxieties are much quicker to rouse than our creativity. We cannot provide overnight cures to the ailments of 20th century communities.

Sometimes the fastest way to do something well is rather slow. Ultimately, it's worth every minute.

This document addresses the emergence of generative communities by looking at what they are, what conditions support their flourishing, and what concrete practices can nurture their further development. In addition, separate sections look at the skills for individual community members to be generative and support generative communities, and the cosmological context within which this paradigm shift can be better understood.

In other words, The Way of Generativity is about why we need to nurture generativity in ourselves and our communities, and how we can begin to do that today. It is not an intellectual formula; it is a common framework and language as an aid for doing the work.

Made in the USA
San Bernardino, CA
14 February 2018